The Real Presence of Christ in the Liturgy and in the World

Anne Y. Koester

LTP
LITURGY
TRAINING
PUBLICATIONS

Nihil Obstat
Deacon David Keene, PHD
Chancellor
Archdiocese of Chicago
August 8, 2023

Imprimatur
Most Rev. Robert G. Casey
Vicar General
Archdiocese of Chicago
August 8, 2023

The *Nihil Obstat* and *Imprimatur* are declarations that the material is free from doctrinal or moral error, and thus is granted permission to publish in accordance with c. 827. No legal responsibility is assumed by the grant of this permission. No implication is contained herein that those who have granted the *Nihil Obstat* and *Imprimatur* agree with the content, opinions, or statements expressed.

Acknowledgments continued on page 72.

Cover art by Cody F. Miller; illustration compositing by Juan Alberto Castillo.

Interior illustrations on pages iv and viii by James B. Janknegt; page 14 by Michelle Wood; page 30 by Laura James; and pages 44 and 58 by Cody F. Miller. Chapter icons and flame graphic by Juan Alberto Castillo © Liturgy Training Publications.

This book was edited by Danielle A. Noe, MDIV. Michael E. Novak was the production editor, Juan Alberto Castillo was the designer, and Kari Nicholls was the production artist.

28 27 26 25 24 1 2 3 4 5

Printed in the United States of America

Library of Congress Control Number: 2023945907

ISBN: 978-1-61671-732-2

PRO

CONTENTS

Blessed indeed is [God's] Son,
present in our midst
when we are gathered by his love,
and when, as once for the disciples,
so now for us,
he opens the Scriptures and breaks
the bread.

—Eucharistic Prayer for Use in Masses for Various Needs:
The Church on the Path of Unity

Introduction

"Present" is the first word spoken by individuals asking to be recognized as catechumens (those seeking baptism) in the Catholic Church.[1] It is a striking response as they are called by name in the midst of the baptized assembly and take the first ritual step toward initiation into the Body of Christ. It's much more than "Hey, I'm in the building." In the presence of the community, they answer God's summons to enter into relationship with God through Christ. They publicly express their desire to learn to know and follow Christ. These individuals exclaim "Present!" as they encounter the presence of Christ in the Church gathered for worship. The assembly reveals Christ to these catechumens and pledges to accompany them on their journey to a shared life in Christ.

Imagine if all of us would shout "Present!" in response not only to Christ present in worship but to our *daily* encounters with Christ, as well. It might be our first word upon waking and the last word of our day, the beginning of our prayer; our first utterance as we call the kids to breakfast and see them off to school; our sacred word as we walk our dog and greet our neighbors; our mantra as we arrive at our workplaces; our punctuation in our texts and social media postings; our response when we encounter someone in need of kindness; our word of gratitude when we are grasped by Beauty; our participation in creation's hymn of praise; our answer when we are confronted with injustice; our exclamation as we gather for Sunday Mass. At the deepest level, "present" is our response to the presence of God revealed in Christ. The abiding presence of Christ is gift. *We* don't initiate or create this presence; it all comes from God, including our capacity to respond to and share this gift.

1. This takes place during the Rite of Acceptance into the Order of Catechumens; refer to the *Rite of Christian Initiation of Adults* (RCIA), 50 (option B). Readers should note that at the time of this printing, a new translation of the RCIA is pending approval from the Holy See.

We are not always as attentive or open to Christ present among us as we are invited to be. We get distracted and sometimes overwhelmed by busyness and the daily demands of life; by cell phones with all their apps, rings, and pings; by our digital culture with its social media postings, videos, advertisements, and news alerts. For some, illness, grief, the effects of abuse and violence, financial hardship, and other worries can leave people feeling adrift. We were also faced in recent years with a global pandemic which, for many, led to distancing and isolation. Many experienced an "online presence" like never before, as people connected with family, friends, coworkers, and classmates on their screens. For Catholics around the globe, although certainly not all, it became commonplace to watch Sunday Mass livestreamed or prerecorded. The full implications of this for an assembly that was mostly absent from a physical worship space and "present" online for an extended period will invite our reflection for years to come.

Our attentiveness to the myriad of ways in which we encounter the presence of Christ is necessary to our ongoing transformation and to that of the world. Our encounters with Christ, our openness to and reflection upon these encounters, lead us to become more Christlike. As people who are continuously being shaped through these encounters, we reveal Christ to the world. Others encounter Christ *in us.*

Our Eucharistic celebrations help us to attend to and to be more conscious of the presence of Christ in our liturgical celebrations *and importantly, in the liturgy of life.* This mutual presence—Christ present to us, the Church present to Christ—shapes our way of being in life. Our lives become a reflection of Christ.

One of the many gifts of the Second Vatican Council is the recovery of a broader understanding of the presence of Christ. The Council's vision is captured in *Sacrosanctum concilium,* which begins with this extraordinary statement: "Christ is always present in his

Church."[2] Yes, that's us! We who are baptized are the Church—in which Christ is always present. The Council goes on to say that Christ is especially present in the Church's liturgical celebrations and identifies a fourfold manner of this presence in the Mass: in the person of his minister, under the eucharistic elements, in his Word, and in the Church gathered for worship, that is, the liturgical assembly.[3]

This resource is an invitation to explore and reflect upon these modes of Christ's presence as articulated by the Second Vatican Council. To do this, we will look at some of the biblical and theological foundations of our understanding of Christ's presence in the Church and our liturgical celebrations, particularly the Mass. We will consider the necessary interplay between the fourfold presence of Christ in the Mass and his presence in the Church and the world in which we live. Because the Church's liturgy is a system of symbols that mediate our experience of Christ, we will include some reminders about the nature of symbols and why we need them. Questions for reflection and discussion are suggested to encourage readers to share their experiences and insights and to feel inspired—compelled, in fact—to live as people soaked in the Sacred Presence, who manifest Christ's presence in the liturgy of life.

2. *Sacrosanctum concilium* (SC), 7.

3. See SC, 7.

Christ is always present . . . especially in its liturgical celebrations. . . . when the Church prays and sings, for he promised: "Where two or three are gathered together in my name, there am I in the midst of them" (Matthew 18:20).

—*Sacrosanctum concilium*, 7

CHAPTER 1

The Assembly

Remarkable, isn't it? Every Sunday, here comes the Church! Or as the author James Joyce wrote, "Catholic means here comes everybody!"[1] We make our way from the various places we call home to the house for the Church. We bring with us all the living we do from Sunday to Sunday. We arrive with our inherent goodness, our acts of compassion and generosity, and our experiences of the many graced moments of our days. We come with our distractions, imperfections, pettiness, and doubts. We who are self-absorbed and at times thoughtless are welcomed alongside the self-giving and attentive. We sometimes take along our complacency, resistance to change, or indifference to the cries of our planet. We have in our back pockets our opinions, political views, personal tastes, and interests. Some of us arrive with health concerns, financial uncertainties, or worries about children. In the mix are the overworked, the job seekers, and those living from paycheck to paycheck. Our sisters and brothers who are grieving cross the threshold of the church, perhaps walking in quiet despair or with throbbing loneliness. The broken-hearted and dispirited enter this

The joys and the hopes,
the grief and anguish
of the people of our time,
especially of those who
are poor or afflicted,
are the joys and hopes,
the grief and anguish
of the followers of Christ
as well.

—*Gaudium et spes*, 1

1. James Joyce, *Finnegan's Wake* (New York: Viking Press, 1939), 32.

liminal (an in-between) space, looking to make sense of life. With all this life stuff, how *present* are we as we gather? How attentive are we to the presence of Christ in our midst? We are frequently less than present—but we'll work on this, here in this space, in this time of worship when we will encounter in heightened ways Christ's transformative presence.

We who make up this gathering share a common identity in Christ but are incredibly diverse with a delightful assortment of ages, racial and ethnic backgrounds, cultures and ancestral traditions, languages and accents, gender identities and sexual orientations, and abilities and needs. We are indigenous peoples, immigrants and descendants of immigrants, refugees and asylum seekers. We are differently abled and bring many talents and skills. We are married and single, widowed and divorced, ordained and vowed religious. The catechumens and others looking for a faith community approach with caution, not yet certain about whether they belong. So too the Catholics who are finding their way back to the Church—with measured steps. We come remembering those who are absent because of illness, work, imprisonment, or other burdens. And yes, here in our diversity, Christ unites us as one body. It's humbling, bewildering, and inspiring all at the same time. Every Sunday when the Church gathers for Eucharist we should be prepared to be amazed!

It's risky, isn't it? After all, we have a standing invitation for conversion of life. Christ calls us to bring our vulnerable selves, our authentic selves that we spend a lifetime discovering. We should come ready to be stripped of our online personas. The AI apps that fascinate us won't do the work we need to do here. Our claims to a particular social status, level of authority or affluence, and job title fall away. In this gathering, such concerns are not what matter. We need to turn off our phones, for the "fear of missing out" on what the liturgy has to say to us is of greater concern than the fear of missing out on the latest postings on our devices. We are invited to trade our daydreams for the reality of Christ truly present to us. We may be awakened to our interconnectedness with the cosmos. We will pray in this space with people we enjoy and those we don't like, people who are like-minded and those with whom we disagree, people we want to hang with and those we try to ignore because they make us uncomfortable. We come to Sunday Mass because we need to be fitted with sacramental glasses so we are better able to see the innate goodness of this world and all who live in it. When we look through these lenses, we see that there are no privileged places, no VIP seats in the Body of Christ. Rather, we see that we are equal in our oneness with Christ. Our sacramental glasses also help us to look within and begin to see ourselves in the way God sees us. We discover that when we surrender to Christ's love expressed through our shared worship, our self-concern is transcended. We embrace the continuous process of being molded into the image of Christ.

Those who have received the grace of baptism are not saved as individuals alone, but as members of the mystical body, having become part of the People of God.

—*Dies Domini*, 31

It's our responsibility, isn't it?—to show up, to be present to one another and to the web of creation we are part of, and to meet Christ, who makes our presence possible. It's our responsibility to be and become more fully who we are—the Body of Christ. It's our responsibility to live out our common priesthood by joining our self-offering to the self-offering of Christ. It's our responsibility to absorb into every fiber of our being that which we are named—the Church. It's our responsibility to present the gifts of our lives so these gifts may be transformed and shared abundantly with humanity and the cosmos, "our common home."[2] You might ask, "Now just *when* did I sign up for all of this?" Simply put, it all began with baptism, when through a ritual action we were claimed for Christ, incorporated into

2. *Laudato Si'*, 1.

the Church, and took on the most significant role of our Christian lives, our first ministry—to be the Body of Christ. From that moment, we are called to live a shared life with Christ. We assume the responsibilities of acting as the liturgical assembly and living as Christian disciples. Our regular participation in the Eucharist, where we meet Christ in profound ways, nourishes and sustains us for this work.

The assembly is essential to our Eucharistic celebrations—a liturgical "must have." Christ's presence in the Church as it gathers to pray and sing is the foundation for the other ways in which Christ is present—in the Word, the sacrament of the Eucharist, and the ordained minister. Our role as assembly is vital to the celebration *and* consequential for our own lives and the life of the world. Our self-understanding as the Body of Christ gathered for the liturgy of the Church and incarnate in the liturgy of the world is fundamental to who we are. It's our daily vocation. It's the basis for our ability to shout "Present!" as we meet Christ in our celebrations of the Eucharist and in our everydayness.

Reclaiming What Was Lost

Our understanding about the assembly's role and the presence of Christ in the Church gathered is rooted in the liturgical life of the early Church. Importantly, these early believers understood themselves as *assembly,* translated as "Church" in the New Testament. For example, in the Acts of the Apostles. the community of believers at Jerusalem is referred to as "church."[3] The baptized throughout Judea, Galilee, and Samaria are likewise identified as "church," which was "being built up and walked in the fear of the Lord, and with the consolation of the holy Spirit it grew in numbers."[4]

Writing to the Corinthians, St. Paul identifies the Church with the one Body of Christ that participates in the Body and Blood

3. Acts of the Apostles 8:1.

4. Acts 9:31.

of Christ through its sharing of the one loaf and the one cup.[5] The Church's oneness with Christ and one another in the Body of Christ was symbolized in this sharing. As we know, divisions within the community threatened this communion, but Paul won't have it. He bluntly warns the Corinthians that as a result of their divisions, their meetings as Church were not a celebration of the Lord's Supper.[6] He impresses upon them that they are one body united with Christ in their sharing of the Eucharist, and through this communion, they "proclaim the death of the Lord until he comes."[7] We further learn from Paul that those who are baptized into Christ become a new creation and "ambassadors for Christ, as if God were appealing through us."[8] The baptized "have clothed" themselves in Christ and are "one in Christ Jesus."[9] The Body of Christ, the Church, says Paul, is the "fullness of the one who fills all things in every way."[10] These powerful images invite our contemplation, for our shared life with Christ through baptism and the Eucharist is undeniable.

Because the loaf of bread is one, we, though many, are one body, for we all partake of the one loaf.

—1 Corinthians 10:17

Last, the writer of Matthew's account of the Gospel points to the community's appreciation of Christ present in their act of assembling for worship—"where two or three are gathered together in my name, there am I in the midst of them."[11]

Assembly as essential to Christian identity and to the celebration of Eucharist is likewise emphasized in other early writings. In the second century, the writer of the *Didache* calls upon Christians

5. See 1 Corinthians 10:16–17.
6. See 1 Corinthians 11:18–21.
7. 1 Corinthians 11:26.
8. 2 Corinthians 5:20.
9. Galatians 3:27–28.
10. Ephesians 1:23.
11. Matthew 18:20.

to gather on the Lord's Day to break bread and give thanks.[12] St. Justin Martyr, an early Christian theologian and philosopher, writes about the role of the assembly in welcoming the newly baptized and in his account of Christian Eucharist. He describes the newly baptized joining the assembled community where prayers were offered and they greeted one another with a kiss. [13] With the newly baptized, the entire assembly shares the Eucharist, bread and drink that has become the Body and Blood of Christ and that nourishes and transforms their own body and blood.[14] Justin stresses the importance of Sundays, when all gather in one place. The memoirs of the apostles and writings of the prophets are read, the presider exhorts the assembly to imitate what they heard, and they all stand together to offer prayers. In response to the presider's prayers and thanksgiving over the bread and cup of water and wine, the assembly gives consent with an "Amen" before all share in the Eucharist. Justin notes that absent members of the assembly were not forgotten; deacons ensured that a portion of the Eucharist was brought to them. Finally, members of the assembly contributed to the collection to assist those in need.[15]

The church, which is [Christ's] body, [is] the fullness of the one who fills all things in every way.

Ephesians 1:22–23

As Christian communities grew, the baptized were not always mindful of their central role in Eucharistic celebrations. In the *Didascalia of the Apostles*, bishops of the third century are advised to teach the people to be faithful to gathering for Eucharist on the Lord's Day, for if they are absent, they "diminish the Church,

12. See "Didache," XIV.1, in *Worship in the Early Church: An Anthology of Historical Sources*, vol. 1, ed. Lawrence J. Johnson (Collegeville, MN: Liturgical Press, 2009), 40.
13. See "First Apology," LXV, in *Worship in the Early Church: An Anthology of Historical Sources*, vol. 1, ed. Lawrence J. Johnson (Collegeville, MN: Liturgical Press, 2009), 67.
14. See "First Apology," 68.
15. See "First Apology," 68.

thus causing the Body of Christ to lack a member."[16] Failing to assemble scatters the Church and scatters Christ's Body.[17] John Chrysostom, preaching in the late fourth and early fifth centuries, reminded the people that "the priest does not give thanks alone but all the people join him in doing so. [Let] us not refer everything to the priest, but we also care for the whole Church as being a body common to us."[18]

From these compelling insights we learn the following:

- Assembly is critical to our self-understanding as a baptized community.
- As Church, we are the one Body of Christ. Our union with Christ and all of creation is symbolized in our sharing of the Eucharist.
- Through baptism, we become a new creation for we become one in Christ Jesus. We take on the role of ambassadors for Christ, "as if," in Paul's striking words, "God were appealing through us."[19]
- The baptized assembly is the fullness of Christ. Christ takes shape in us as we grow through our relationships with Christ, one another, and the created world.
- We learn from the Gospel according to Matthew that Christ is *present* in our very act of assembling for worship.

Taking our cues from the Christians of the early Church, we appreciate that we are called to be faithful to gathering on the Lord's Day to pray, to offer thanksgiving, to share and be nourished and transformed by the sacred food and drink. Without us—*without any one of us*—the Church would be diminished. The Body of Christ would be scattered.

---

16. "Didascalia of the Apostles," XIII, in *Worship in the Early Church: An Anthology of Historical Sources*, vol. 1, ed. Lawrence J. Johnson (Collegeville, MN: Liturgical Press, 2009), 233.
17. See "Didascalia of the Apostles," 233.
18. "Homily" 18, in *Worship in the Early Church: An Anthology of Historical Sources*, vol. 2, ed. Lawrence J. Johnson (Collegeville, MN: Liturgical Press, 2009), 185.
19. 2 Corinthians 5:20.

The assembly's vital role in the Church's liturgy slipped away in later centuries. The clergy assumed the primary role in the Church's liturgical celebrations. The original sense of liturgy as the work of the people was eclipsed by complex ceremonies that were the work of the clergy. The assembly became alienated and passive. The understanding of the baptized as the Church, the Body of Christ visible at Eucharist and in the world disappeared. The focus of Christ's presence at Mass was primarily on the bread and wine. The assembly's participation in the Eucharistic meal became infrequent. Consequently, the Pauline image of the communion between Christ and his Body symbolized through the sharing of Eucharist was weakened.

The Second Vatican Council reintroduced us to ourselves, so to speak. The Council reclaimed and spotlighted the early Christian images of baptized believers as the assembly, the Church. St. Paul's metaphor of the Church as the Body of Christ was reinserted into our vocabulary and into our consciousness. The vital role of the assembly at Mass was recovered. The appreciation that Christ is truly present *in us* as we gather as Church and that this presence is foundational to the layered presence of Christ in our eucharistic celebrations was—*and is*—placed before us as an ongoing invitation to celebrate and live more fully as the Body of Christ.

Encountering the Presence of Christ

All of this leads to the question, "In what ways do we encounter Christ in the assembly gathered for Eucharist?" We can all answer this question, and our answers will be as diverse as we are. Each of us can tell stories about our experiences of encountering Christ in the assembly that are unique to us as persons, but at the same time we can give voice to what we hold in common as a community. And more than likely, our stories will be different in some ways from week to week, because we are different from week to week. We do a lot of living from Sunday to Sunday, and are continuously shaped and reshaped by our meeting Christ in our daily experiences. So, who we are and what we bring every Sunday is not the same every time we arrive for Eucharist.

Assembling

Our assembling begins with an invitation—one that has always existed and at the same time is unceasingly renewed. God invites us as the Body of Christ into a holy assembly, to be named, to be visible, and to become more fully who we are, recognizing that we will remain incomplete in this life. As persons who are baptized (and those seeking baptism), Christ is already present and taking shape within each of us and within our community. Meeting Christ in the Eucharistic assembly amplifies what we already know to be true—that Christ is present in us and the world in which we live.

As we make our way to the place of gathering, are we attentive to our own sacredness? Do we as individuals take seriously that we have been claimed for Christ and thus bear the imprint of Christ? Granted, there are probably weeks when we come more conscious of the patterns in our lives that obscure rather than reflect Christ's indwelling. But that's why we're here. The Eucharist calls us to conversion of life and is the primary sacrament of healing.

> **The Church's mission stands in continuity with the mission of Christ: "As the Father has sent me, even so I send you" (John 20:21).**
>
> —*Ecclesia de Eucharistia*, 22

Becoming more attuned to Christ's presence in ourselves will help us better see Christ in our coworkers in the assembly. At the same time, our openness to meeting Christ in them can lead us to a deeper meeting of Christ within ourselves and frames how we meet the Sacred in all persons and in the whole of creation. How important it is then to "take in" our gathering—to be present to Christ present in each of us and in us as Church. It just might take our breath away!

Christ present in us and in our act of gathering is expressed through our hospitality. We embody the hospitality of Jesus Christ. Do we reflect the heart of Christ in our words and actions? Do we honor the dignity of every person who gathers with us, knowing that in them we meet Christ? Do we show our sisters and brothers who are marginalized, carry heavy burdens, feel unsure about God's love for them that they belong here? Do we see others as Christ sees them? Do we meet Christ in them and they in us? This conscious meeting of Christ in those with whom we gather on Sundays will enable us to meet Christ in the people whose lives merge with ours in our homes, schools, workplaces—whenever and wherever we live out our life of faith.

Doing Our Work

Christ accomplishing in us the work of assembling, of extending and receiving hospitality, is the beginning of what happens at Sunday Mass. The presence of Christ in and through us becomes known in the many ways we carry out our work as the Eucharistic assembly, as this work is mysteriously united with the work of Christ. There's no easing into this work or looking on from the sidelines while others participate. Our work is immediate as we plunge our fingers into the baptismal font, sign ourselves with the same words with which we were baptized, and bow or genuflect toward the altar.[20] We then stand and in one voice, sing the entrance song while also aware of simultaneous movements as we get a whiff of incense, see the processional cross held high, observe the *Book of the Gospels* carried forward to the altar, and unite ourselves in prayer with the presider and all the liturgical ministers. The purpose of these symbolic actions is to awaken us to the presence of Christ in our midst. Christ is revealed to us as we engage in this work that is ours by baptism.

Assured of Christ's mercy and forgiveness, we bring to mind ways in which we fall short of living up to our name as the Body of

20. If the tabernacle is present in the sanctuary (typically behind the altar), we genuflect. If the tabernacle is in another location (such as a Eucharistic chapel), we bow to the altar.

Christ. We surrender to the healing presence of Christ, as we humbly call out, "Lord, have mercy," "Christ have mercy," "Lord, have mercy." Through this ritual act, Christ invites us to be transformed and become visible signs of the mercy, forgiveness, and healing that Christ offers. We are now better prepared to meet Christ at the Table of the Word.

Christ's presence in the gathered Church continues to take shape as we encounter Christ in the Liturgy of the Word. We are on the edge of our seats, eager to meet Christ in the stories of Scripture, and in the readers who have encountered Christ in their preparation and proclamation of the readings. We prayerfully sing the responsorial psalm, while the Word penetrates our hearts and minds. We stand as we are able, eyes fixed on the *Book of the Gospels* as we sing the Gospel acclamation. Our encounter with Christ is deepened as the Good News is proclaimed and we recognize the presence of Christ in the priest or deacon who "serves up" the Gospel passage. It's a profound intersection of the modes of Christ's presence—in the assembly, the Word, and the minister. Our presence intertwined with Christ's presence fashions us into what we have been named, and by our attitudes and actions in the world we continue to proclaim God's Word, the Good News.[21] We in whom Christ is truly present become the Good News to a world in need of hope. This, too, is our work given to us in baptism and renewed in the Eucharist.

Like the first witnesses of the resurrection, Christians who gather each Sunday to experience and proclaim the presence of the Risen Lord are called to *evangelize and bear witness* in their daily lives.

—*Dies Domini*, 45

Our encounter with Christ in the Word proclaimed and broken open in the homily leads us to recite the creed, our statement of

21. See chapter 5 in this book.

common beliefs held by Christians through the ages. This is our responsibility as Church, made very clear for us when we "give" the creed to the elect who are preparing for initiation at Easter. We hand on to them and invite them into the faith we cherish and live. We then carry out our priestly duty by lifting up our needs and the needs of others in the universal prayer.

Our awareness of Christ present in us is sharpened as we do the work of preparing the Table of the Eucharist. We present simple gifts of bread and wine that symbolize the sacramentality of our creation, the work of human hands, and the giving of ourselves. We stand as one with the risen Lord, one another, and creation. We pray the Eucharistic Prayer, joining our prayer and self-offering with the prayer and self-offering of Christ present in the priest. We pray that these ordinary gifts of the earth and human work be transformed into the extraordinary, the Body and Blood of Christ—to which the Body of Christ at the Table sings "Amen!"

We ready ourselves to share in the sacrament of unity with Christ and all of creation by praying in one voice for what we need to carry out our work of discipleship, and we receive and offer the peace that Christ freely gives to us. We fall into the Communion line with our sisters and brothers in Christ—we who are the broken and healed, the stumbling and holy move forward in procession, step by step on our journey toward God. We each receive the same amount of bread, the same amount of wine. We say "Amen" ("I believe!") to who we are and become what we receive—the Body of Christ, the Blood of Christ. We also receive the same mandate—to be Eucharist in the world. We are to be bread for the hungry, people who willingly share our lives with others. We share in Christ's cup of suffering and become people willing to be poured out for those who cry out, including the earth. It's who we are—a people made for living in communion with the entire human family and all of creation.

Before we move out into the larger community, we hear these words of invitation that we have heard a few times already: "The Lord be with you." We are asked again to affirm that as the Church gathered,

Christ is present *in us* and working *through us*. It sets us up for what comes next—"Go and announce the Gospel of the Lord" or "Go in peace, glorifying the Lord by your life." Our work continues.

Do any of us really understand this?

Well, no—at least not fully. But we live this mystery as people who trust in God's promises, as people who get glimpses and nudges, as people who encounter Christ daily, who get bowled over by the Holy Spirit when we are inattentive. We learn to trust the slow work of God—we try it on and become who God knows us to be. Christ is truly taking shape in us.

For Discussion and Reflection

1. **What strikes you about the early Christian understanding of the assembly gathered for Eucharist?**
2. **Without us—any one of us—the Church would be diminished and the Body of Christ would be scattered. What do you think about this statement?**
3. **What are your stories about the ways in which you experience the presence of Christ in the Sunday assembly?**
4. **What insights does this chapter offer you about your role as assembly at Mass and your baptismal responsibility to be Body of Christ in the world?**

[Christ] is present . . . in the person of his minister. . . . By his power he is present in the sacraments, so that when a man baptizes it is really Christ himself who baptizes.

—*Sacrosanctum concilium*, 7

CHAPTER 2

The Minister

One of my classmates during my theology studies was a Benedictine monk and priest from Uganda. We quickly became good friends and remain so twenty-five years later. If you were to meet my friend, Fr. Gabe, I think you would first notice his infectious joy. It's evident in his warmth and laughter, the absolute delight he takes in being with people, his hopeful outlook and reassuring words that flow out of a deep faith formed by prayer, Scripture reflection, liturgy, work, and daily interactions with the world around him. His humility, listening heart, giving spirit, and an imagination that is receptive to encountering Christ in the ordinary are also readily apparent. There is a transparency about Fr. Gabe that allows others to meet Christ in him. He practices a self-forgetfulness and leads a life of gratitude, praising God as the source of all that is good.

> **Look for Christ our Lord in everyone and you will then have respect and reverence for all.**
>
> —St. Teresa of Ávila

These same gifts shine through Fr. Gabe when he presides at Mass. His love and respect for people carries over into his attitude toward the assembly. He honors the presence of Christ in the assembly and recognizes the interdependence of his role and theirs in the liturgy. As he gives voice to the assembly's prayer, he draws attention to Christ and not to himself. He is fully aware that the prayer is not his prayer alone but the action of the whole assembly. His proclamation of the Gospel and his preaching reflect a daily engagement with biblical texts and a pondering of how these texts shed meaning on the lives of the people before him. His strong imagination and attentiveness to the symbolic support the assembly's participation in the liturgy and their receptivity to its transformative power. Fr. Gabe's way of presiding signifies the mutual presence of Christ —he is present to Christ who is present to and through him.

I could tell many similar stories about priests I know, who are likewise effective presiders and compelling preachers. I hope that my observations about Fr. Gabe give us a point of entry into a reflection on the presence of Christ in the minister.[1]

Convergence of Priesthoods

In the liturgy, there is a convergence of priesthoods. Yes, *priesthoods* —plural. We speak in the Church about the priesthood of Christ, the baptismal or common priesthood, and the ministerial priesthood. These priesthoods are closely related to one another and are interwoven with the modes of Christ's presence in the Mass. Let's take a look at what we understand about these priesthoods to help us appreciate more fully the presence of Christ in the minister when we gather for Eucharist.

The Priesthood of Christ

"You are a priest forever in the line of Melchizedek."[2] Chances are this verse from Psalm 110 rings familiar. We sing these words as our responsorial psalm on the Solemnity of the Most Holy Body and Blood of Christ (Year C). On the same Sunday, Melchizedek shows up in the first reading. Other than having a great name, what do we know about him? We learn from Genesis that Melchizedek was king of Salem (an ancient name for Jerusalem) and a "priest of God Most

1. The reflections here about the presence of Christ in the minister are focused on priests. However, what is said here also applies when the presiding minister is a bishop, for bishops and priests are "two degrees of ministerial participation in the priesthood of Christ" (*Catechism of the Catholic Church*, 1554).
2. Psalm 110:4b.

High."[3] He blessed Abram upon his return from battle with the kings who kidnapped Abram's nephew, Lot.[4] Melchizedek is portrayed in the story as having brought bread and wine with him,[5] an action read in the Christian tradition as a foreshadowing of the Eucharist. The writer of the Letter to the Hebrews interprets Melchizedek as a prefiguration of Christ.[6] This is the basis for the Church's teaching that Jesus Christ is the fulfillment of everything that the priesthood of the Old Covenant prefigured; he is the "unique 'high priest after the order of Melchizedek'" and the "one mediator between God and" humanity.[7]

"You are a priest forever in the line of Melchizedek."

—Psalm 110:4b

Catholics understand the liturgy, which unites us with Christ, as an "exercise of the priestly office of Jesus Christ."[8] His self-offering "by the unique sacrifice of the cross"[9] is "accomplished once for all"[10] and yet made present in our celebration of the Eucharist. We further understand that the priesthood of Christ is made present through the ministerial priesthood, although this does not take away from the uniqueness of Christ's priesthood.[11]

The Baptismal and Ministerial Priesthoods

In 2017, I heard Dominican priest and theologian Gerard Austin accept the prestigious Berakah Award, presented by the North American Academy of Liturgy, in recognition of Fr. Austin's

3. Genesis 14:18. Genesis 14:18–20 is proclaimed on the Solemnity of the Body and Blood of Christ (Year C).
4. See Genesis 14:12–16.
5. See Genesis 14:18.
6. See Hebrews 7.
7. *Catechism of the Catholic Church* (CCC), 1544.
8. SC, 7.
9. CCC, 1544.
10. See CCC, 1545.
11. See CCC, 1544 and 1545.

scholarship, teaching, and ministry.[12] A story he told illustrates the relationship between the baptismal and ministerial priesthoods. Fr. Austin said that while in the seminary in the 1950s, he was trained "to think of 'priesthood' only in terms of ordained clerics."[13] He added that he had not yet understood the baptismal theology of the early Church and the priestly nature of the Church itself, and admitted that he saw the Church as having "first and second-class citizens: the first-class being the clerics, the ordained."[14] Five years after his ordination and during doctoral studies that introduced him to a reclaimed and renewed baptismal theology, Fr. Austin did a "flip-flop" in this thinking.[15] He came to realize that the most important day of his life was the day of his baptism, not the day of his ordination as he had previously believed.[16] It became clear to him that the Church is a communion and that all members have in common "a sharing in the divine life and a participation in the priesthood of Christ."[17] He came to recognize that his ministerial priesthood is fundamentally linked with his participation in the priesthood of Christ that began with baptism.

Almighty God, the
Father of our Lord
Jesus Christ,
has freed you from sin,
given you new birth
by water and the
Holy Spirit,
and joined you to
his people.
He now anoints you
with the Chrism
of salvation,
so that you may remain
members of Christ,
Priest, Prophet
and King,
unto eternal life.

—*Order of Baptism of Children*, 62

12. See "The Berakah Award," as found on the North American Academy of Liturgy website, accessed December 7, 2022, https://www.naal-liturgy.org/about/berakah/.
13. Proceedings, North American Academy of Liturgy Annual Meeting 2017, 38.
14. Proceedings, 38.
15. See Proceedings, 38–39.
16. See Proceedings, 39.
17. Proceedings, 39.

We have likely heard the words spoken during the baptism of infants, when the minister anoints the child with Sacred Chrism and says, "[God] anoints you with the Chrism of salvation, / so that you may remain as a member of Christ, Priest, Prophet and King, / unto eternal life."[18] Through baptism, we share in Christ's mission as priest (mediator between God and humanity), prophet (messenger who gives witness to God and calls people to turn toward God), and king (leader who brings peace and justice) and in the priesthood of Christ, which "provides the basis for communion with all Christians."[19] We live out our baptismal or common priesthood by living out of our baptism and shared life with Christ. The journey is an "unfolding of baptismal grace—a life of faith, hope, and charity, a life according to the Spirit."[20]

> **Through the ordained ministry, especially that of bishops and priests, the presence of Christ as head of the Church is made visible in the midst of the community of believers.**
>
> —*Catechism of the Catholic Church*, 1549

As Fr. Austin's remarks make clear, the ministerial priesthood begins with the immersion into the priesthood of Christ at the moment of baptism. The baptismal priesthood and the ministerial priesthood, while "'ordered one to another'" are at the same time different.[21] How so? The "ministerial priesthood is at the service of the common priesthood" and "is directed at the unfolding of the baptismal grace of all Christians."[22]

We further understand that Christ's presence as the Head of the Body—that is, the baptized—is made visible through the service of the ordained minister.[23] Through the sacrament of Holy Orders,

---

18. *Order of Baptism of Children*, 62.
19. *Compendium of the Catechism of the Catholic Church*, 263.
20. CCC,1547.
21. CCC, 1547.
22. CCC, 1547.
23. See CCC, 1549.

the priest acts in the person of Christ the head (*in persona Christi capitis*).[24] The priest is a sacramental sign of Christ as the Head of the Body. Ordained ministry "depends entirely on Christ and on his unique priesthood," and therefore, the exercise of this role is "measured against the model of Christ."[25]

> **[In the liturgy] the prayers addressed to God by the priest, who presides over the assembly in the person of Christ, are said in the name of the entire holy people and of all present.**
>
> —*Sacrosanctum concilium*, 33

The ordained minister also acts "in the name of entire holy people and of all present" when we gather to celebrate the Eucharist.[26] Note, however, that this "does not mean that priests are the delegates of the community," because the Church's prayer and offering are joined with the prayer and offering of Christ and Christ always "worships in and through his Church."[27] In other words, the entire assembly prays in and with the person of Christ because of their baptismal priesthood. The presiding minister prays "in persona Christi capitis—that is, as the one sacramentally representing the headship of Christ in the common prayer of the Body."[28] Through the ordained minister then, as he proclaims the mystery of Christ, the assembly's offering is united with the sacrifice of Christ, the Head of the Body.[29]

24. See CCC, 1548.
25. CCC, 1551.
26. SC, 33.
27. CCC, 1553.
28. Paul J. Philibert, "Reclaiming the Vision of an Apostolic Church," *Worship* 83:6 (2009) 493–494. See also *Catechism of the Catholic Church*, 1553: "It is because the ministerial priesthood represents Christ that it can represent the Church."
29. See *Lumen gentium*, 33.

The Presence of Christ

The convergence of priesthoods adds another dimension to the layered presence of Christ in our Eucharistic celebrations. They are threads of the same cloth. With this in mind, let us reflect in particular on our encounters with the presence of Christ in the minister.

Gathering

I can still hear my theology professor, Fr. Kevin Seasoltz, OSB, ask, "*Who* is the host of the Eucharist?" For emphasis and clarity, he would immediately answer his own question, "*Jesus Christ* is the host!" He was unambiguous about who summons the community—and it isn't us! Christ invites us to gather. In response, the priestly people assemble; the Body of Christ is visible. The ordained presider, aware of Christ present in the gathered Church and through his service, makes visible to the assembly that Christ has called them to this celebration. In what ways is this made known to us in the action of the Introductory Rites?

> **The Church must be a place of mercy freely given, where everyone can feel welcomed, loved, forgiven and encouraged to live the good life of the Gospel.**
>
> —*Evangelii gaudium*, 114

Think of times when the ordained minister embodies Christian hospitality as people cross the threshold of the doors of the church into the gathering space. We encounter the presence of Christ in the minister through his awareness of the sacredness of the people and his welcome to all who enter as Christ welcomes all. It's a ministry like that of St. Alphonsus Rodriguez, who was the doorkeeper for a Jesuit school in seventeenth-century Spain. Whenever he heard a knock on the door, he would say to himself, "I'm coming, Lord!" Like Alphonsus, the ordained minister (and indeed, *each of us*) is called to be present to and reverence the presence of Christ in every person who arrives at the Church's doorstep.

We can also point to the procession, as the ministers move forward in the midst of the gathered Church, where Christ is present, and into a liminal space. In this space, we encounter the transformative power of Christ acting in and through the community's worship and will be returned to everyday living not the same as we were before. Christ's invitation into this time of liminality becomes concrete in the ordained minister as he moves in procession toward and reverences the altar, and *sees* and *hears* Christ present in the assembly. The minister's way of seeing, hearing, and acting in these moments is discernable to the holy people gathered and bids them to recognize the presence of Christ in him.

Pope Francis emphasizes that for the service priests do as liturgical presiders to be well done, they must have "a keen awareness of being, through God's mercy, a particular presence of the risen Lord,"[30] and because the ordained minister is one of the ways in which the Lord is present, the Christian assembly is made unique. This gives "'sacramental' weight" to all the gestures and words of the presider and the assembly "has the right to be able to feel in those gestures and words the desire that the Lord has, today as at the Last Supper, to eat the Passover with us."[31] The ordained minister "should be overpowered by the desire for communion that the Lord has toward each person."[32]

> **To preside at Eucharist is to be plunged into the furnace of God's love.**
>
> —*Desiderio desideravi*, 57

Filled with the desire for communion that the Lord has toward those gathered, the minister greets the members of the Body of Christ and invites them to enter into the prayer of Christ: "The

30. *Desiderio desideravi* (DDes), 57.
31. DDes, 57.
32. DDes, 57.

grace of our Lord Jesus Christ, / and the love of God, / and the communion of the Holy Spirit / be with you all." The Body of Christ extends the same in response: "And with your spirit." This brief but powerful exchange points to the complementary nature of the priest and the assembly and again to the layered presence of Christ at Mass with Christ present in the gathered Church and in the ordained minister.

As our worship continues, the minister invites us to encounter the abiding love and healing presence of Christ. Reassured, we recall the patterns in our lives when we have failed to be faithful to our baptism and shared life with Christ. The minister gives voice to our need for forgiveness and asks for God's merciful love to enfold us—"May almighty God have mercy on us, / forgive us our sins, / and bring us to everlasting life"— to which we say, "Amen!" The minister then bids the assembly to praise God for all God has done and continues to do in Jesus Christ and the Holy Spirit by singing the Gloria, which leads to the collect of the day. The gestures and words of the minister in these opening rites carry "'sacramental' weight"[33] and when done with humility and self-forgetfulness, they draw attention to Christ. We are able to *see* Christ through the one who sacramentally represents Christ as the Head of the Body. In this way, the ordained minister places himself at the service of the baptismal priesthood and supports the "unfolding of the baptismal grace"[34] of all who are present.

Liturgy of the Word

As the assembly is seated, we might again be conscious of the intensity of Christ's presence that envelops us and summons our presence as we enter into the Liturgy of the Word. Christ is present in the people and is actively shaping them more and more into the Body of Christ as they listen and ponder the Word that is broken open for the salvation of the world. Christ is present in the Word proclaimed,

33. DDes, 57.
34. CCC, 1547.

preached, and lived. And Christ is present in the ordained minister as the sacramental sign of the headship of Christ as he attends to the Word, proclaims the Gospel passage, and carries out his "sacred duty of preaching the Gospel."[35]

Through the readings and homily, Christ's paschal mystery is proclaimed; through the sacrifice of the Mass it becomes present. Moreover Christ himself is also always present and active in the preaching of his Church.

—*Introduction, Lectionary for Mass*, 24

Let us look more closely at the ways in which Christ's presence as the Head of the Body is visibly expressed through the service of the minister during the Liturgy of the Word. First, Christ is visibly present in the minister's posture and attitude of *listening*. As the Body of Christ is called to do, he actively listens to the readings proclaimed and encounters Christ in the Scriptures, in the deacon, readers, and psalmists who proclaim it, and in the listening assembly being formed by the Word. The minister's encounter with Christ's presence in these ways *shapes him* more and more into the sacramental sign of Christ's headship.

As the cantor intones the Gospel acclamation and the minister participates in the Gospel procession, the presence of Christ is visible in his reverence of the *Book of the Gospels* and of the people who stand before him, eager to hear the Good News. As with the greeting at the beginning of the Mass, he both expresses his awareness of the Lord's presence in the Body of Christ and invites the assembly into

35. *Presbyterorum ordinis*, 2. Throughout this chapter, the focus has been on the priest. However, Christ is also present in the ministry of the deacon. A deacon, who serves God's people in communion with the bishop and priests, is a visible sign of the relationship between sharing in the Eucharist and service. At Mass, a deacon assists in various ways, including proclaiming the Gospel, and the deacon may preach the homily. The deacon voices the needs of the people in the general intercessions, helps receive the offerings of the people and prepare the gifts, supports the full, conscious, and active participation of the people during the Eucharistic Prayer, extends the invitation of peace, serves as the ordinary minister of the Blood of Christ during Communion, and sends the assembly with the mandate to live the Gospel. See the *National Directory for the Formation, Ministry, and Life of Permanent Deacons in the United States*, 33 and 35.

their own awareness of the Lord present in their midst—"The Lord be with you." The Body of Christ, again faithful to their own priesthood in Christ, extends the same in response—"And with your spirit." We encounter Christ's presence in the proclamation of the Gospel, for in the Word proclaimed and in the one who proclaims, we meet Christ. We also meet Christ in the minister because we assume he has met Christ in the kind of prayerful engagement with the text that is needed to "serve up" the Word and preach a homily that sheds light on the meaning of the Scripture texts and the liturgy itself.

A primary duty and privilege of the ordained minister is to preach. He speaks the concerns of the community and "represents the Lord by offering the community another word, a word of healing and pardon, of acceptance and love."[36] As preacher, the minister points to the ways in which God's ongoing presence in the world is made known. To do this effectively, the preacher needs "to be a listener before he is a speaker."[37] He is called to "a prayerful dwelling"[38] with the people and the sacred texts, which enables him to listen to the Lord's voice in the Scriptures and in the daily lives and experiences of those whom he serves. Out of the "dialogue between the Word of God in the Scriptures and the Word of God in the lives of [the] people, the Word of God in preaching begins to take shape."[39] Ultimately, the homily leads the Body of Christ to celebrate the liturgy "more deeply and more fully—more faithfully—and thus be formed for Christian witness in the world."[40]

People often say that a homily on a given day "really spoke to me." They likely mean they found the stories, images, or insights particularly relevant to their own experiences as people of faith living in a complex world. Perhaps the preacher's words renewed their spirit, reassured their troubled hearts, or challenged them to think

36. *Fulfilled in Your Hearing* (FYH),13.
37. FYH, 20.
38. FYH, 23.
39. FYH, 20.
40. FYH, 43.

and act differently. This happens when, as Pope Francis says, the preacher keeps "his ear to the people"[41] and contemplates both the Word and the people. It also reflects that the preacher understands that his role is to draw attention not to himself but to the many ways Christ meets us in the ordinariness of life.

Liturgy of the Eucharist

We enter into the Liturgy of the Eucharist with the procession of gifts and the minister's reception of these gifts. Are we present to what happens here? Members of the assembly, transformed by their encounter with Christ present in the Word, move forward with the bread and wine (and perhaps food or money for those in need) and with great care place them in the minister's hands. We also encounter in this symbolic action the offering of our own lives. The minister, in whom Christ's presence as the Head of the Body is visible, receives then not only the assembly's offering of bread and wine, but also the offering of themselves. He receives the bread and wine knowing that these gifts will become the Body and Blood of Christ, the sacred food that will strengthen the identity of the baptized as the Body and Blood of Christ in the world. And he receives the assembly's gift of their availability as they join in the self-offering of Christ. This is a powerful moment. Through his sacramental role, the minister makes concrete the mystery that Christ receives the assembly's offering of the things of the earth that will become sacred food and the offering of their very lives that will become the nourishment that is Christ for the world.

Through the ministry of the priests, the spiritual sacrifice of the faithful is made perfect in union with the sacrifice of Christ.

— *Presbyterorum ordinis*, 2

41. *Evangelii gaudium*, 154.

The minister blesses the assembly's gifts and prays silently, "With humble spirit and contrite heart / may we be accepted by you, O Lord, / and may our sacrifice in your sight this day / be pleasing to you, Lord God." The minister may then incense the bread and wine, pointing to the presence of Christ in the Eucharistic action and the altar, a symbol of Christ. The minister himself is incensed by a deacon or acolyte, which further draws attention to the presence of Christ in the minister. Finally, the deacon, acolyte, or server honors the presence of Christ in the assembly with a profound bow and the sweet-smelling incense.

> **The power to administer the sacrament of the Eucharist . . . is always a service to God's people.**
>
> — *Evangelii gaudium*, 104

The minister, praying in persona Christi capitis and proclaiming the Eucharistic Prayer, joins the offering of the baptized assembly with the sacrifice of Christ, the Head of the Body. He prays that God send the Holy Spirit upon the gifts of bread and wine "so that they may become for us / the Body and ✝ Blood of our Lord Jesus Christ."[42] He prays too that we who will be nourished by the Body and Blood of Christ and "filled with his Holy Spirit / may become one body, one spirit in Christ."[43] As the assembly is formed through these words and actions, the minister too is "formed by presiding over the words and by the gestures that the Liturgy places on his lips and in his hands."[44] Pope Francis stresses that in the Eucharistic Prayer, during which the offering of Christ in the Last Supper is remembered, the minister "participates with the offering of himself," for he "cannot say, 'Take this, all of you and eat of it, for this is my Body which will be given up for you,' and not live the same desire to

42. Eucharistic Prayer II.
43. Eucharistic Prayer III.
44. DDes, 60.

offer his own body, his own life, for the people entrusted to him."[45] Through the minister's own self-offering, the Church meets the presence of Christ.

We are also invited to encounter Christ in the minister's words and gestures that extend the peace of Christ to all who are gathered, and the assembly offers the same in response. This exchange sparks a broader sharing of the peace Christ gives within the assembly, where the presence of Christ is continuing to take shape.

Filled with desire for the communion that the Lord has toward the assembly and present to Christ in the people, the gifts of bread and wine transformed, and in himself, the minister invites the baptized to the Table to receive and be named what they are—the Body and Blood of Christ.

Sending Forth

The minister expresses his awareness of Christ's presence in the Body of Christ as we are ready to go out and announce the Good News. He invites the assembly to be conscious of Christ present in them—"The Lord be with you." In response, the people, who have been renewed and nourished, extend the same to the minister—"And with your spirit." As the sacramental sign of the Head of this Body, the minister blesses the assembly and gives us our mandate—"Go in peace, glorifying the Lord by your life."

45. DDes, 60.

For Discussion and Reflection

1. **Revisit the opening story about Fr. Gabe (see page 15). Do you have a similar story to tell about an ordained minister? What qualities do you see that make him an effective presider and compelling preacher?**
2. **What are your thoughts about the complementary nature of the baptismal or common priesthood and the ministerial priesthood?**
3. **Recall experiences you have had of the Mass when you met the presence of Christ in the ordained minister. What in particular lingers for you?**

[Christ] is present in his word, since it is he himself who speaks when the holy Scriptures are read in the Church.

—*Sacrosanctum concilium*, 7

CHAPTER 3

The Word of God

We arrive at Mass with our overscheduled lives, from our homes or places of work or, for some, temporary shelters or makeshift beds on the streets. We greet one another, say a few words to catch up on the past week, embrace those we haven't seen in some time or those who need comfort. A greeter extends a worship aid, along with "Good morning!" We find a place to sit, first reverencing the altar, a symbol of Christ, with a bow.[1] As the community settles in, there's a prayerful silence. The cantor welcomes us—this holy gathering, the Body of Christ that has assembled, where Christ is truly present. The entrance song is announced, the assembly stands as they are able and joins in the singing. There might be the sweet aroma of incense as the procession of ministers begins. They move forward on behalf of us all, marking the journey of faith we share. As we sing, the processional cross comes into view, led by the rising smoke of the burning incense. A deacon, or if one is not present, a reader, carries aloft a beautiful book. The artistry is apparent with elegant lettering and images that adorn the *Book of the Gospels* (also called an Evangeliary). This book is placed on the altar where, after we feast at the Table of the Word, the sacred meal will be prepared. The presiding minister, in whom Christ is truly present, reverences the altar with a profound bow and kiss and takes his place, ready to lead the assembly in prayer. Already we see gestures of reverence toward the Word that call us to attend to the presence of Christ. Note the layering of presence—in the Body of Christ assembled, the

1. If the tabernacle is present in the sanctuary, we genuflect instead.

presiding minister, in the Word symbolized by the *Book of the Gospels* and in the readers and priest or deacon prepared to proclaim the sacred texts. The lively interaction of these modes of Christ's presence is clear. All of this in the first few minutes of Mass!

The Word through History

Before continuing with our liturgical imagining and our focus on the many ways in which we encounter Christ in the Word, let's take a brief look at the emphasis on the Word in Christian worship practices in the early Church period, the shift in focus that came about in later centuries, and the renewed prominence of the Word in Catholic worship since the Second Vatican Council. This historical snapshot will hopefully lead to a deeper appreciation of the importance of the Word in our worship, our Church, and our daily lives.

In the beginning was
the Word,
and the Word was
with God,
and the Word was God.
He was in the beginning
with God.
All things came to
be through him,
and without him
nothing came to be.
What came to be
through him was life,
and this life was
the light of the
human race;
the light shines in
the darkness,
and the darkness has
not overcome it.

—John 1:1–5

New Testament Communities

We begin with St. Paul, who himself experienced a life-changing encounter with Christ. His conversion story is well known. The risen Lord spoke to him, and his heart and mind were opened. Paul was baptized and at once proclaimed Jesus as the Son of God.[2] He spoke of his vocation as preaching the Gospel, the Good News of Jesus Christ. He wrote to the Romans that he had been "set apart for the

2. See Acts 9:1–20.

gospel of God, which he promised previously through his prophets in the holy scriptures, the gospel about his Son."[3] In this same letter, he declared that he was "not ashamed of the gospel. It is the power of God for the salvation of everyone who believes."[4] Paul told the Ephesians that the mystery of Christ had been "revealed to his holy apostles and prophets by the Spirit" and declared them "coheirs, members of the same body, and copartners in the promise in Christ Jesus through the gospel."[5] We see here an instinctive sense that the mystery of Christ was encountered through the telling of the stories about his life, death, resurrection, and ascension and that the baptized shared in the gift of salvation offered through this encounter. The First Letter of Peter movingly expresses the enduring nature of the Word of the Lord:

> You have been born anew, not from perishable but from imperishable seed, through the living and abiding word of God,
>
> for:
>
> "All flesh is like grass
> and all its glory like the flower of the field;
> the grass withers,
> and the flower wilts;
> but the word of the Lord remains forever."
> This is the word that has been proclaimed to you.[6]

The evangelist Luke tells the story of the risen Christ walking with two disciples on their way to Emmaus. He *stayed* with them and the disciples recognized him in the sharing of food and Word:

> And [Jesus] said to [his disciples], "Oh, how foolish you are! How slow of heart to believe all that the prophets spoke! Was it not necessary that the Messiah should suffer these things

3. Romans 1:1–3a.
4. Romans 1:16.
5. Ephesians 3:5–6.
6. 1 Peter 1:23–25.

> and enter into his glory?" Then beginning with Moses and all the prophets, he interpreted to them what referred to him in all the scriptures. As they approached the village to which they were going, he gave the impression that he was going on farther. But they urged him, "Stay with us, for it is nearly evening and the day is almost over." So he went in to stay with them. And it happened that, while he was with them at table, he took bread, said the blessing, broke it, and gave it to them. With that their eyes were opened and they recognized him, but he vanished from their sight. Then they said to each other, "Were not our hearts burning within us while he spoke to us on the way and opened the scriptures to us?"[7]

We find in the Acts of the Apostles that the first Christians were summoned to gather and they "devoted themselves to the teaching of the apostles and to the communal life, to the breaking of the bread and to the prayers."[8] The teaching of the apostles—the Good News of Jesus Christ—was central to their life and worship. Christ was present among them in their gathering, the telling of the stories, their prayer, and the breaking of bread.

The Early Church

The second-century Christian philosopher Justin Martyr described early Christian Eucharistic gatherings in his *First Apology,* in which he observed:

> [O]n the day that is called Sunday all who live in the cities or in rural areas gather together in one place, and the memoirs of the apostles or the writings of the prophets are read for as long as time allows. Then after the lector concludes, the president verbally instructs and exhorts us to imitate all these excellent things.[9]

---

7. Luke 24:25–32.
8. Acts 2:42.
9. "First Apology," LXV, in *Worship in the Early Church: An Anthology of Historical Sources*, vol. 1, ed. Lawrence J. Johnson (Collegeville, MN: Liturgical Press, 2009), 68.

As it was with the New Testament communities, the "memoirs of the apostles" (the Gospel accounts) and the writings of the prophets (as found in the Old Testament) had a central role in early Christian worship. Moreover, the presider urged the assembly *to live* what they heard. Notably, the sacred readings preceded the preparation and sharing of the Eucharistic meal. Participating at the Table of the Word led to participating at the Table of the Eucharist.

Tertullian, a Christian writer in the late second and early third centuries, spoke of gathering to read the sacred writings and believed that "with the holy words we nourish our faith, enliven our hope, strengthen our trust, and no less by teaching God's precepts we strengthen our way of life."[10]

An early sixth-century bishop, Caesarius of Arles, preached about the value of the Word of God, noting that it "is not worth less than the Body of Christ":

> We take such great care when Christ's Body is given to us so that nothing of it might fall from our hands onto the ground. We are to be just as careful that God's word, which is given us, not perish from our hearts while we are thinking of speaking about something else.[11]

A Shift in Emphasis

As the Church moved into the Middle Ages the proclamation of Scripture lost its place of prominence in Christian liturgy. The Eucharistic elements of bread and wine became the focus, which unfortunately overshadowed the role of Sacred Scripture and the sense of encounter with the presence of Christ in the Word. This led to an imbalance in the celebrations, with fewer Scripture readings and a greater emphasis on the Eucharistic elements. There was no longer the same understanding that earlier Christians had that the

10. Johnson, "Apology," XXXIX, *Worship in the Early Church*, vol. 1, 68.
11. "Sermon 78," in *Worship in the Early Church: An Anthology of Historical Sources*, vol. 4, ed. Lawrence J. Johnson (Collegeville, MN: Liturgical Press, 2009), 108.

sacred meal they shared was in response to the sharing of the stories and instructions on the teachings.

The Recovery of the Word of God

Fast forward to the scholarship of the nineteenth and twentieth centuries, which brought a rediscovery of the ancient roots of Christian liturgy, as well as new methods of biblical studies in the Catholic Church. This extraordinary work paved the way for the reforms of the Second Vatican Council (1962–1965), the Council out of which the Church lives today. The Council restored the rightful place of Scripture in the Church's liturgy and emphasized Christ's presence in both Word and sacrament.

> **When the word of Scripture is proclaimed . . . it is not a new message but a new challenge.**
>
> —*In Spirit and Truth*, 23

To appreciate the Council's vision, we look first to the *Sacrosanctum concilium*. This document provided the framework for the reforms of the Church's liturgy, including all of its sacramental celebrations, which were introduced in the years after the Council and which continue to unfold today. In this document, the Council made clear the essential place of Scripture in liturgy:

> Sacred Scripture is of the greatest importance in the celebration of the liturgy. For it is from Scripture that the readings are given and explained in the homily and that psalms are sung; the prayers, collects, and liturgical songs are scriptural in their inspiration; it is from the Scriptures that actions and signs derive their meaning.[12]

We see here a comprehensive approach to the place of Sacred Scripture in liturgy. Yes, it's certainly about the Scripture readings proclaimed, the psalms that are sung, the preaching that invites

12. SC, 24.

deeper reflection, and the living out of what we hear and sing. But it's also about the prayers and songs that are inspired by and receive their power from Scripture and about the many liturgical actions and sacred signs that draw their meaning from Scripture. The Word of God from Scripture permeates all aspects of Catholic liturgy.

The Council specifically instructed that the "treasures of the Bible are to be opened up more lavishly, so that a richer share in God's word may be provided for the faithful."[13] With this, the Council sought to rebalance the Church's liturgy:

> The Church has always venerated the divine scriptures as it has venerated the Body of the Lord, in that it never ceases, above all in the sacred liturgy, to partake of the bread of life and to offer it to the faithful from the one table of the word of God and the Body of Christ.[14]

We are nourished by Jesus Christ, the Bread of Life,[15] at *both* tables, the Table of the Word and the Table of the Eucharist.

> **The people of God have a spiritual right to receive abundantly from the treasury of God's word. Its riches are presented to them through the use of the Order of Readings, the homily, and pastoral efforts.**
>
> —*Introduction, Lectionary for Mass*, 45

Catholics today are familiar with the *Lectionary for Mass*. The three-year Sunday Lectionary was introduced with the reforms to the Church's liturgy in the late 1960s and early 1970s.[16] Its purpose is to provide the rich fare of biblical readings to the baptized assembly at the Table of the Word as envisioned by the Council. Every ritual book of the Church is published with an introduction. The introductions include theological reflections on the liturgical rite as well as basic norms for its celebration. The *Introduction* to the *Lectionary for*

13. SC, 51.
14. *Dei verbum*, 21.
15. See the Bread of Life discourse in John 6:22–59.
16. The Catholic Church also has a two-year lectionary for weekday Masses.

Mass emphasizes the significance of the Word in Catholic liturgy, noting that the liturgical celebration is "founded primarily on the word of God and sustained by it" and "becomes a new event and enriches the word itself with new meaning and power."[17] The *Introduction* stresses that Christ is always present in his word[18] and that "the faithful should be keenly aware of the one presence of Christ in both the word of God—it is he himself 'who speaks when the Sacred Scriptures are read in the Church'—and 'above all under the Eucharistic species.'"[19] Finally, the *Introduction* urges that when the gathered Church hears and reflects upon the word of God, they "are enabled to respond to it actively with full faith, hope, and charity through prayer and self-giving, and not only during Mass but in their entire Christian life."[20]

The intimate connection between the liturgy of the word and the liturgy of the Eucharist in the Mass should prompt the faithful to be present right from the beginning of the celebration, to take part attentively, and to prepare themselves in so far as possible to hear the word, especially by learning beforehand more about Sacred Scripture.

—*Introduction, Lectionary for Mass*, 48

Encountering Christ in the Word

With this background in mind, we return to our liturgical imagining and our experiences of encountering Christ in the Word. We already recalled the assembly gathering, the entrance procession, and the gestures of reverence toward the Word that call us to attend to the presence of Christ. We also noted the necessary and dynamic interplay between the modes of Christ's presence in our Sunday

17. *Introduction, Lectionary for Mass* (ILM), 3.
18. ILM, 4.
19. ILM, 46.
20. ILM, 48.

celebrations that awakens us—*enables us to be present*—from the very beginning of Mass.

While we might want to go immediately to the Liturgy of the Word to reflect on our experiences of encountering Christ's presence in the Word, let us not overlook the entrance song, the presider's greeting, the invitation to reflect on our failings and proclaim "Lord, have mercy, Christ, have mercy, Lord, have mercy," the singing of the Gloria, and the collect as inspired by Scripture.[21] Each of these elements enfolds us in God's Word and invites us to be present to Christ.

From here, our encounter with Christ in the Word intensifies. The assembly is seated and assumes a posture of *active* listening,[22] open to the possibility of hearing something that could lead to a change of attitude or a new way of acting. A reader moves to the ambo, a place of proclamation and preaching. We meet Christ here—in the reader, a member of our community, for we assume they have met Christ in their preparation to proclaim the Word. When a lector or reader sits with the text, ponders it, and becomes aware of Christ's presence in the passage, their proclamation will allow us to see Christ through their ministry. They reveal Christ to the assembly as they read the text, as they "serve it up"[23] for the Church to discover and respond to Christ

> **There are two ways of keeping God's word, namely, one whereby we store in our memory what we hear and the other, whereby we put into practice what we have heard.**
>
> —Bl. Jordan of Saxony

21. See SC, 24.
22. We listen in different ways. Some need the words of our liturgy to be signed; others need the acoustics of a worship space to be conducive to hearing with aids that amplify sound. How do we support the listening experience for all members of the assembly?
23. This phrase is borrowed from the late Bishop of Saginaw, Michigan, Kenneth E. Untener. His point was that lectors ought to proclaim the reading with conviction but avoid a dramatic reading that risks drawing attention to themselves and distracting listeners from encountering the presence of Christ in the biblical text.

present in the word. They conclude with the pronouncement "The Word of the Lord," to which we say, "Thanks be to God!"

The first reading we hear proclaimed is most often from the Old Testament; the exception is during Easter Time when we hear from the Acts of the Apostles. The Catholic Church teaches that in proclaiming both testaments, we are "proclaiming one and the same mystery of Christ" because:

> The New Testament lies hidden in the Old; the Old Testament comes fully to light in the New. Christ himself is the center and fullness of the whole of Scripture, just as he is of all liturgical celebration.[24]

The first reading leads us to sing a responsorial psalm, an "integral part of the Liturgy of the Word,"[25] which we recognize as another way of God speaking to us. These psalms become the prayer of the Church,[26] of *us*, the Body of Christ assembled.

We continue our participation in the Liturgy of the Word as a reader "serves up" the second reading, taken from a book of the New Testament.[27] We are invited again into this encounter with Christ in the Word—through the reader, through the sacred text. As with the first reading, the reader names what has been proclaimed as they conclude the passage with "The word of the Lord." Our response? "Thanks be to God!" Do we *really* hear what we are saying? Are we truly attentive to what we say, or has it become rote? We express our deep gratitude to God for reaching out to us in relationship through the Word who is incarnate in Jesus Christ.

Suddenly, the silence after the second reading is broken by the singing of the "Alleluia!" or another verse, depending on the liturgical season. It is the assembly's greeting of welcome "to the Lord who

---

24. ILM, 5.
25. *General Instruction of the Roman Missal* (GIRM), 61. This document serves as the introduction to the third edition of *The Roman Missal* and provides theological reflections on the meaning of the Mass as well as the norms and directions for celebrating the Mass.
26. See ILM, 19.
27. We hear from Acts of the Apostles, the letters, and epistles in the second reading.

is about to speak to them and as an expression of their faith through song."[28] We stand as we are able, poised again to encounter Christ truly present. Our symbolic actions at this moment draw further attention to our reverent stance before Christ as we prepare to encounter him in the Gospel. There is again a procession, the deacon or priest walking to the altar and lifting high the *Book of the Gospels*; he is led by incense and flanked by lit candles, the flames flickering as the assembly sings and the Gospel reader moves to the ambo. The deacon or priest greets the assembly with "The Lord be with you," to which we say, "And with your spirit." He announces, "A reading from the holy Gospel according to . . . ," signs the text on the page with the sign of the cross, and signs his own forehead, lips, and heart while saying inaudibly, "Cleanse my heart and my lips, almighty God, / that I may worthily proclaim your holy Gospel." We again signal our recognition of Christ present, "Glory to you, O Lord," and as has been the custom for decades now in many places, we too sign our forehead, lips, and heart. As it was with the other readers, we encounter Christ in the Gospel reader, as we assume he has met Christ in his own preparation to proclaim the text. As the passage is concluded, we hear "The Gospel of the Lord." Note that this pronouncement is similar to what we heard earlier—"The word of the Lord"—and functions in the same way. And to this pronouncement we say, "Praise to you, Lord Jesus Christ." We again give voice to our encounter with Christ, truly present—and speaking to us!—in the Gospel proclaimed. The proclamation of the Gospel calls us forth from the liturgy to *live* the Gospel, the Good

> **[The Alleluia] serves as the greeting of welcome of the assembled faithful to the Lord who is about to speak to them and as an expression of their faith through song.**
>
> —*Introduction, Lectionary for Mass*, 23

28. ILM, 23.

News, in the world in which we live. Others may then encounter Christ's presence in our words and actions; we reveal Christ in what we say and what we do. Thus, the *Book of the Gospels* is not carried out in the recessional as we conclude Mass. When we go forth, glorifying the Lord by our life, it is we who proclaim the Good News by giving witness to Christ in the world.

Our encounter with the presence of Christ in the Word continues with the homily, so the "spoken word of God and the liturgy of the Eucharist may together become 'a proclamation of God's wonderful works in the history of salvation, the mystery of Christ.'"[29] We believe that Christ is present and active in the preaching of the Church. This presence is then what shapes and transforms us as we take in what is preached.

From Sunday to Sunday the word of the Risen Lord illuminates our existence, wanting to achieve in us the end for which it was sent.

—*Desiderio desideravi*, 65

In response to the Word of God, we pray in a united voice the symbol of faith, the creed. Illuminated by God's Word, the assembly then prays

1. for the needs of the Church;
2. for public authorities and the salvation of the whole world;
3. for those burdened by any kind of difficulty;
4. [and] for the local community.[30]

With these petitions, "'the people, exercising their priestly function, make intercession for all,'"[31] and with the full effects of the Liturgy of the Word realized, the assembly is better prepared for the Liturgy of the Eucharist. Indeed, as St. Jerome teaches us:

29. ILM, 24, quoting the SC, 35, 2.
30. GIRM, 70.
31. ILM, 30.

The Lord's flesh is real food and his blood real drink; this is our true good in this present life: to nourish ourselves with his flesh and to drink his blood in not only the Eucharist but also the reading of Sacred Scripture. In fact, the Word of God, drawn from the knowledge of the Scriptures, is real food and real drink.[32]

For Discussion and Reflection

1. **How do you prepare yourself to listen to the Word of God and be open to the presence of Christ?**
2. **In what ways does your parish enable all persons to participate in the Word through listening? Are there unaddressed needs in this regard?**
3. **In what ways do you embrace your identity as members of the baptized Body of Christ and proclaim the Good News of Christ in your daily life?**
4. **Do you sign your forehead, lips, and heart when the Gospel is announced? What meaning does this ritual gesture have for you?**

32. As referenced in *Instrumentum laboris*, 35.

[Christ] is present in the sacrifice of the Mass . . . especially under the eucharistic elements.

—*Sacrosanctum concilium*, 7

CHAPTER 4

The Sacrament of the Eucharist

The COVID-19 pandemic was, plainly speaking, hard. *Very* hard. An unimaginable number of people died or endured sickness. It impacted all facets of our global society. Life as we knew it was upended, and it quickly became apparent that there would be no returning to what was or to "normal," for we had all been through too much to be left unchanged by the experience.

Of course, faith communities were not untouched by all of this. They needed to find creative ways to continue to be available to people. For Catholics, concern for the health and safety of one another meant not gathering for Sunday Mass and other occasions. Many parishes scrambled to figure out ways to use technology to livestream Mass. In places where this was not available or in homes where people were unfamiliar with online tools, Catholics found other ways to keep Sunday, perhaps praying alone or with family. The Sunday liturgical assembly seemed scattered. We listened to the Word online or read the passages on our own. Those who were able to go to Mass were not able to receive from the cup. The rest of us fasted completely from the Eucharistic meal for months to avoid large gatherings and the spread of the virus. Our presence *to* the presence of Christ in our Sunday celebrations was challenged. A primary means of rehearsing us to readily recognize Christ in our daily lives as well as for participating in the heavenly banquet felt muted or at least different.

Not all was lost; after all, Christ is everywhere and always. We encountered Christ in many and various ways as we took care of ourselves and others, tried to do our jobs and go to school, reached out to neighbors, and prayed our way through this distressing time. Our physical absence from Sunday Mass hopefully led to a deeper yearning to be nourished at the Table of the Word and the Table of the Eucharist, an increased longing to encounter Christ in the assembly gathered in a sacred space, and a greater appreciation for what we as Church do at Sunday Mass and why we need to do it.

Particularly poignant for Catholics during the pandemic were the Sundays they were unable to experience the real presence of Christ in the Eucharistic meal and say "Amen" to the offering of the Body and Blood of Christ. Obviously, sharing bread and wine through a computer or TV screen was not an option. We came to know a profound hunger and thirst. This is not to say that the diminished experience of Christ's presence in the assembly, the presiding minister, and the Word was not also keenly felt, for it was. As previously noted, there is an essential interplay among the modes of the presence of Christ. At the same time, there is a distinctive character about Christ's presence in the Eucharistic elements of bread and wine.

As health conditions allowed, we returned to assembling for Sunday Mass. The experience of the pandemic and our return to gathering in person for liturgy present a valuable opportunity to reflect on the mystery of the Eucharist and specifically on our encounter with Christ's risen presence in the sacrament. To guide our reflection, we will look to the biblical foundations of Eucharist and the understandings of early Christians. From there, we will probe our own encounters with the presence of Christ in the Eucharist.

The Eucharist through History

Biblical Foundations

We turn first to St. Paul, who gives us the earliest written account of the Christian Eucharist. Paul received the tradition of the Eucharist from a community of Christians he visited early in his mission and handed on this tradition to others, including the Christians at Corinth. We know this from his first letter to the Corinthians, in which he addressed pastoral problems in the community concerning the Eucharist. Paul had to remind the Corinthians that their sharing of the bread and cup brought about a *real participation* in the Body and Blood of Christ. Their sharing of this meal was more than a social fellowship. It brought about an intimate and life-giving communion with Christ and one another. Through their participation, they shared life with Christ and with all who shared this same life in the Body of Christ. Their consumption of Eucharistic Bread and Wine transformed them into one community, united with Christ and one another.

> The cup of blessing that we bless, is it not a participation in the blood of Christ? The bread that we break, is it not a participation in the body of Christ? Because the loaf of bread is one, we, though many, are one body, for we all partake of the one loaf.[1]

Paul confronted the Corinthians about the divisions within the community, which were contrary to the meaning of Eucharist. He used the words from their own liturgy to remind them of Jesus' actions at the Last Supper:

> For I received from the Lord what I also handed on to you, that the Lord Jesus, on the night he was handed over, took bread, and, after he had given thanks, broke it and said, "This is my body that is for you. Do this in remembrance of me." In the same way also the cup, after supper, saying, "This cup is the new covenant in my blood. Do this, as often as you drink it, in remembrance of me." For as often as you eat this bread and drink the cup, you proclaim the death of the Lord until he comes.[2]

1. 1 Corinthians 10:16–17
2. 1 Corinthians 11:23–26.

This narrative from early Christian liturgy expresses Jesus Christ's complete giving of himself; Christ becomes food for us. He gives his very life for us—"my body that is for you"[3] and his Blood (his *life*) that forms a new covenant. God is a giving God. This divine giving is embodied in Jesus Christ and is present in every celebration of the Eucharist. As did the Corinthians, we encounter this divine giving in the bread and wine that become part of our very being as individuals and as a community. Through our participation in the Body and Blood of Christ, we experience God with us and in us, and through this sharing in the divine life, we become one body. When we are truly present to these realities, we cannot help but be self-giving in the manner of Jesus. *This* is what we do in memory of him.

In the Gospel accounts, Jesus feeds the hungers of the people who encounter him, nourishing them with his teachings and the food only he could give. Consider, for example, the feeding stories. The crowds were like "sheep without a shepherd."[4] He taught them, healed the sick among them, and fed their deepest hungers as he took, blessed, broke, and gave food to them. "They all ate and were satisfied."[5] Even then, the food Jesus gave was not depleted; their encounter with Jesus was an encounter with God's lavish and perpetual giving.

I am the bread of life; whoever comes to me will never hunger and whoever believes in me will never thirst.

—John 6:35

Jesus sat at table with those no one else wanted to sit with—the marginalized and forgotten, the poor and oppressed, the sick and suffering, the haughty and despised, the foolish and sinful. Jesus taught, healed, and forgave during meals.[6] He was present to them and invited *all* persons into relationship with himself through this

3. 1 Corinthians 11:24.
4. Mark 6:34.
5. Mark 6:42.
6. See Mark 6:22–44; Mark 8:1–10; Matthew 14:13–21; Matthew 15:21–28; Luke 9:10–17; John 6:1–15.

table ministry, where food and life were shared. His actions affirmed their value and dignity as persons created and loved by God. For those who wanted to be healed, their encounter with Jesus brought new life.

On the night he was betrayed, Jesus shared a ritual meal with his disciples. The Last Supper narratives in the synoptic Gospel accounts (Matthew, Mark, and Luke) echo the actions of Jesus in the feeding stories.[7] He took, blessed, broke, and gave them food that would draw them into deeper relationship with himself and one another, food that would provide ongoing sustenance. He declared the bread his Body, "which will be given for you,"[8] and the wine his blood of the new covenant, "which will be shed for you,"[9] and invited his disciples to eat and drink. "Do *this* in memory of me."[10] In John's version of the Last Supper, we find not the words of institution of the Eucharist as in the synoptics; rather, we see Jesus wash feet and command those who believe in him to do likewise.[11] "Do this in memory of me."[12] Washing feet was not a one-off grand gesture; rather, Jesus' humble service flowed out of his entire life. His act of self-giving in the midst of the sacred meal firmly joined Eucharist and service of all of God's creation.

After the resurrection, the disciples encountered the risen Christ mediated through daily concrete experiences. Recall the story of Christ walking with the disciples on their way to Emmaus. The disciples recognized him when at table—he took, blessed, broke, and gave bread to them.[13] Through this encounter, their eyes were opened. In John's Gospel account, Christ revealed himself to the disciples fishing in the Sea of Tiberias. On their own, they caught nothing. When they encountered Christ, they caught an abundance of fish. The disciples came ashore to find Christ making breakfast.

7. See Mark 14:22–26; Matthew 26:26–30; Luke 22:14–20.
8. Luke 22:19.
9. Luke 22:20.
10. Luke 22:19; emphasis added.
11. John 13:1–15.
12. Luke 22:19; emphasis added.
13. See Luke 24:30.

They realized it was the Lord when he "took the bread and gave it to them, and in like manner the fish."[14] They encountered the divine mediated through Christ's words, the food he shared, and his abundant self-giving. As the disciples experienced the absence of the earthly Jesus, they encountered the ongoing presence of the risen Christ. He would be with them always "until the end of the age"[15] and would send an Advocate, the Spirit of Truth.[16]

From this very brief look at the biblical foundations of the Eucharist, we can say the following:

- Jesus was *present* to all who encountered him in his earthly mission through his generous self-giving as he taught, healed, and fed their deepest hungers. He extended welcome to and served *everyone*; he turned no one away from the table nor did he exclude anyone from his invitation to come to life. He gave of himself completely, ultimately giving his life on the cross.
- Jesus' death on a cross did not undermine God's faithfulness. Rather, Jesus' death, resurrection, and ascension brought about new and abundant life for all of God's creation. Through the power of the Holy Spirit, the gift of Christ's life-giving and ongoing presence is offered to all persons. The presence of Christ is a mediated presence; Christ is encountered through the concrete realities of life—through persons and stories, symbols and rituals, history and time, nature, and the entire cosmos.
- We know from Paul's letters that the presence of Christ in the Eucharistic meal shared by Christians was a given. Christ's presence in their liturgy invited their presence and participation, which united them with Christ and formed them into one community. Divisions were intolerable and inconsistent with a true celebration of the Lord's Supper. Christians met Christ in their *koinonia,* their "common-union," and in the Eucharistic elements of bread and wine transformed into the Body and Blood of Christ.

14. John 21:13.
15. Matthew 28:20.
16. See John 16:7–14.

Beyond the New Testament

The real presence of Christ in the celebrating Church and the Eucharistic food became deeply embedded in the Christian imagination. The baptized shared in divine life through their participation in the Church's liturgy and, in a distinct manner, the bread and wine transformed into the Body and Blood of Christ. This is reflected in the powerful catechesis of St. Cyril of Jerusalem:

> Under the figure of bread we receive his Body. Under the figure of wine we receive his Blood. In this way, by sharing in Christ's Body and Blood, we become one Body and one Blood with Christ. In this way we become "bearers of Christ," his Body and his Blood spreading throughout the members of our bodies. And so, according to blessed Peter, we become "sharers in the divine nature."[17]

Similarly, St. John Chrysostom preached that "as the bread, consisting of many grains, is made one, and the individual grains are no longer apparent yet still exist, so too we are joined to one another and to Christ."[18]

> **See what you believe . . . become what you see.**
>
> —St. Augustine

By the ninth century in the western Church, the understanding of Christ's presence in the Eucharist narrowed. The Church shifted away from an appreciation of a layered sense of Christ's presence in the Mass, with Christians encountering Christ in the Word proclaimed and in the action of the assembly, to an almost exclusive focus on Christ's presence under the appearances of bread and wine. Alongside this shift, the assembly's active role in the celebration of the Eucharist and its identity as the Body of Christ fell away. The place of Scripture in the liturgy was

17. "Mystical Catechesis IV," citing 2 Peter 1:4 in *Worship in the Early Church: An Anthology of Historical Sources*, vol. 2, ed. Lawrence J. Johnson (Collegeville, MN: Liturgical Press, 2009), 333.
18. Johnson, "Homily 24," *Worship in the Early Church*, vol. 2, 181.

eclipsed by the intense focus on the Eucharistic elements. Participation in Communion became infrequent, so the physical consumption of the Eucharist, the real sharing in the Body and Blood of Christ was not a regular practice. For many Catholics, Christ seemed distant. Consequently, an awareness that they shared in the divine life through the sharing of Eucharist was lacking. There was a disconnect between the presence of Christ in the Eucharist and everyday life.

> **In this sacrament the consecration of the matter consists in the miraculous change of the substance, which can only be done by God.**
>
> —St. Thomas Aquinas

The nearly exclusive focus on the Eucharistic elements also came about during a time when there was a suspicion about symbol. Christians of earlier generations had a strong symbolic disposition; they were receptive to encountering the mystery of God through words, story, actions, objects, song —that which was visible and tangible and pointed to deeper realities. With such an appreciation, they did not seek to analyze how Christ was present in the Eucharist they celebrated; it was taken for granted. In later centuries, as people sought to prove matters with objective evidence, the symbolic tended to be dismissed. In the Church, theologians sought to prove Christ's presence in the Eucharist by analyzing the nature of the change in the bread and wine. They looked to a branch of philosophy known as metaphysics in their effort to explain this mystery. Applied to the Eucharist, theologians concluded that the change in the bread and wine is at the metaphysical, not physical, level. The underlying essence or substance of the bread and wine changed; the external physical properties of the bread and wine remained. Therefore, when we speak of the "real" presence of Christ in the Eucharist, we are referring to a metaphysical reality. This more limited focus on the real presence of Christ did not consider the presence of Christ in the Church gathered for worship, nor the essential role of the community. Overlooked was the earlier understanding that the people were formed into one Body and shared in the divine life through their participation in the Body and Blood of Christ. Keep in mind that reception of Communion was not a regular experience as it is today.

> **For the liturgy "making the work of our redemption a present actuality," most of all in the divine sacrifice of the eucharist, is the outstanding means whereby the faithful may express in their lives and manifest to others the mystery of Christ and the real nature of the true Church.**
>
> —*Sacrosanctum concilium*, 2

The Second Vatican Council returned us to a broader understanding of Christ's presence in the liturgy, reminding us that Christ is present in more than one way, while also noting the distinctive sacramental presence of Christ in the Eucharist. The Council pointed to Christ's presence in the Word and returned Scripture to its prominent place in liturgy. The Council called attention to the presence of Christ in the minister at Mass and stressed Christ's presence in his Church, the people of God, and in the assembly gathered for worship. Along with this came a renewed emphasis on the vital role of the liturgical assembly and its identity as the Body of Christ.

The Council's teaching on the ways in which Christ is present was influenced by a renewed appreciation of the symbolic nature of liturgy. To speak about Catholic liturgy as a system of symbols can make some of us nervous, particularly if we live in societies that treat symbols as simple "stand-ins" for something else, and therefore not real. Symbols are often thought of as an insertion of characters, scientific shorthand, or a one-tap exclamation in a text message. This superficial understanding fails to communicate the true nature of symbols. We need to shake off this confusion and be open to the inherent power of symbol to participate fully in and be formed by the Church's liturgy. Symbols are fundamental to human life. We are natural symbol-makers, storytellers, and ritual-doers; we speak in metaphors, use images, express ourselves through music, art, and poetry. We cannot truly *live* without symbols. They can pry us open and work us over, lead us to interpret the complexities of life, help us speak the unspeakable, and point us to deeper meanings. Symbols open us up to the Mystery of God and invite us to see, hear, imagine, and speak in new ways. The symbols of the Church's liturgy—from the doors of the church to the assembly; our sacred spaces with font, ambo, and altar; the paschal candle and sacred oils; the gifts of bread and wine; our processions and postures, gestures, and song—are inexhaustible in their meanings, for they are primary symbols of the paschal mystery. Pope Francis has stressed the need to "acquire the interior attitude that will let us use and understand liturgical symbols" so we are not "robbed of such richness."[19]

> The Liturgy does not leave us alone to search out an individual supposed knowledge of the mystery of God. Rather, it takes us by the hand, together, as an assembly, to lead us deep within the mystery that the Word and the sacramental signs reveal to us. And it does this, consistent with all action of God, following the way of the Incarnation, that is, by means of the symbolic language of the body, which extends to things in space and time.[20]

Encountering the Presence of Christ

The Liturgy of the Eucharist begins with preparing the gifts we will place on the altar. Members of the assembly humbly move in procession to the altar, bearing the gifts of bread and wine. Are we present to the symbols we encounter here? The bread and wine, the work of human hands, sacred signs of life and prosperity; the procession and the music that accompanies this movement to the altar, the symbol of Christ; the offering of the gift of our messy but holy lives, for they too are placed on the altar; the minister's reception of these gifts and

19. DDes, 47.
20. DDes, 19.

lifting them up in prayer to give thanks and acknowledge that all comes from God. "Blessed are you, Lord God of all creation, / for through your goodness we have received / the bread [the wine] we offer you . . . / it will become for us the bread of life [our spiritual drink.]" We pray that our sacrifice may be acceptable to God. "Our sacrifice" is joined with the sacrifice of Christ; it's our willingness to expend ourselves, to give totally and freely of ourselves as Christ did.

Following the preface to the Eucharistic Prayer, we join the angels and saints in acclaiming "Holy, Holy, Holy Lord God of hosts!" Our prayer continues with one of the Eucharistic Prayers, in which the priest prays on behalf of us all that God bless the gifts of bread and wine so that they become for us the Body and Blood of our Lord Jesus Christ. We recount the words of Jesus at the Last Supper and are reminded to take and eat, take and drink, and to do this in memory of him. We pray that we "may become one body, one spirit in Christ"[21] as we share in the Body and Blood of Christ. In response to this encounter with Christ in these gifts transformed into his Body and Blood and as we become one in Christ, we say "Amen!"

> **May the Lord accept the**
> **sacrifice at your hands**
> **for the praise and glory**
> **of his name,**
> **for our good**
> **and the good of all his**
> **holy Church.**
>
> —*The Roman Missal*

We pray in one voice that God's kingdom come, God's will be done; we ask that we be given what we need—our daily bread—and that we forgive and are forgiven. All is directed toward building God's reign. We extend to one another the peace that only Christ can give. Christ present in our midst makes this gesture possible as a real sharing in his peace. Do we show up for this gesture and offer Christ's peace that dwells within to those we love, to those we don't

21. Eucharistic Prayer III.

know or don't like, and to those who are unseen or even rejected? Do we extend ourselves in peace within this Body of Christ where Christ is present?

> **[You] are the Body and the members of Christ, your mystery is placed on the Lord's table; you receive your own mystery. Respond "Amen" to what you are.**
>
> —St. Augustine

Aware of Christ's presence in our midst, we ask the Lord to heal us, for it is only then that we are worthy to receive, to take into ourselves the Body and Blood of Christ. As a symbol of our journey to become one with Christ and one another, we move in procession —shuffling our feet, wheeling ourselves forward, carrying children in our arms, tapping our canes or crutches—one by one, the Body moves toward the altar. We come before the Communion minister, priest, deacon, or lay person, seeing Christ present in them, as we are also aware of this same presence in us. We make a "throne"[22] for the Lord in our hand, ready to receive the Body of Christ. We say "Amen" (which literally translates from Hebrew, "so be it!") to the Body of Christ, to the real presence of Christ in the bread transformed into his Body *and* to who *we are*. Following the command of Jesus to eat and drink, we likewise approach the communion minister with the cup, deacon or lay person, and again aware of the profound presence of Christ in the sacred drink and in one another, we are named "The Blood of Christ," to which we can only say "Amen" ("So be it!").

In the Catholic imagination, the presence of Christ in the sacrament does not cease as we depart. This presence continues in the Eucharistic elements and in *us*. Believing the presence of Christ is a continuing presence, we reserve the sacrament in a tabernacle so that we may bring it to the sick. We also invite people to spend time in prayer before the Lord there so they may be drawn more deeply into

22. Johnson, St. Cyril of Jerusalem, "Mystagogical Catechesis V," *Worship in the Early Church*, vol. 2, 337.

solidarity with Christ and the whole of creation. And we go forward from our liturgical celebration as a transformed community—as the Body of Christ broken for sharing with the world, the Blood of Christ for sharing in the world's sufferings.

For Discussion and Reflection

1. **Read the biblical passages referenced in this chapter. What in these texts speaks to you and why?**
2. **Jesus sat at table with an assortment of people. Who are your table companions where you share food and life?**
3. **St. Cyril of Jerusalem said we become "bearers of Christ" as we share in the Body and Blood of Christ. In what ways were you a bearer of Christ today?**
4. **Be attentive to your "Amen" as you receive Communion at Mass. In what ways do you live out your "Amen" to being the Body of Christ in daily life?**
5. **What does it mean that our life of mission comes from the Eucharistic celebration?**

Christ is always present in his Church. . . . Christ always truly associates the Church with himself. . . . The Church is the Lord's beloved Bride who calls to him.

—*Sacrosanctum concilium*, 7

CHAPTER 5

The Body of Christ in the World

It's remarkable, isn't it? Every Sunday, there goes the Church! We are sent, commissioned, told to "go!" We move out, go forth. We just thanked God for our mandate to announce the Gospel, to glorify the Lord by how we live. We are not the same as when we arrived, for we have encountered the transformative presence of Christ throughout our experience of the Eucharistic liturgy. We have been fed at both tables (Word and Sacrament), strengthened in our baptismal identity, and become a little more attuned to Christ taking shape in us. Diverse though we are, we have become more conscious of our oneness in Christ. As one Body, we joined in the prayer, work, and self-giving of Christ. How could we possibly be the same? We are ordinary people repeatedly molded into the extraordinary—the Body of Christ. Through our participation in the Mass, we are gradually fashioned into something new, as though the water in which we were baptized continuously washes over us, smoothing out our rough edges and forming us into a people "clothed" in Christ.[1]

> **For all of you who were baptized into Christ have clothed yourselves with Christ.**
>
> —Galatians 3:27

1. Galatians 3:27.

It's risky, isn't it? This being sent for mission, especially since we move out as people who are not the same as we were. By participating in the Eucharistic celebration, we said "yes" to the invitation to conversion. We brought with us our messy holy lives. We silenced our phones and faced our FOMO[2] anxieties. Concerns about ambitions, influence, and social circles became irrelevant. We were awakened to our interconnectedness with humanity and the entire cosmos. We prayed and shared life with people known and unknown to us. Our sacramental glasses were adjusted and polished. The symbols we encountered may have shaken us up a bit, shed meaning on our lives, encouraged new impulses, and generated fresh insights. We rehearsed our role as the Body of Christ, and the challenge to live as Church in the world was renewed. It's a lot to grasp and yet, every Sunday we say "Thanks be to God" as we are told to go. We can't duck or hide behind our hymnals or dash out the door after Communion to escape being sent (although some try). The mandate is ours as baptized people, as Eucharistic people. Pope Francis reminds us,

> Every liturgical celebration always concludes with the mission. What we live and celebrate leads us to go out towards others, to encounter the world that surrounds us, to encounter the joy and the needs of many who perhaps live without knowing the gift of God. The genuine liturgical life, especially the Eucharist, always impels us to charity, which is above all openness and attention to others.[3]

It's risky because we don't know what the encounters Pope Francis speaks of will be, what our "openness and attention to others" will bring. These encounters with the world, with the joys and needs of people could be hugely inconvenient, upend our plans, decenter us, cause us to reprioritize what we value, even change our

2. Fear of missing out.
3. "Address of His Holiness Pope Francis to Teachers and Students of the Pontifical Liturgical Institute," 7 May 2022, https://www.vatican.va/content/francesco/en/speeches/2022/may/documents/20220507-pont-istituto-liturgico.html.

life! We who wear sacramental glasses see the needs of others more clearly, spot injustices, and feel compelled to act with compassion and generosity. We appreciate more deeply our relationship with all of creation and seek to change attitudes and behaviors that harm the planet. As the Church sent forth, we can't turn away from or forget what we see. In the words of Pope Francis, we who are "fed and nourished by the very body and blood of Christ cannot remain unaffected" when, for example, we encounter those who suffer want and hunger[4] and countless other needs and injustices.

It's our responsibility, isn't it? To show up for the *liturgy of life*, to be present to the sacredness of the world that surrounds us, to become increasingly conscious of meeting Christ in our daily interactions with people and our common home. It's our responsibility to be sacrament, a visible sign of Christ's continuing presence in the world. It's our responsibility to live up to that which we are named—the Body of Christ, the Church, the Word of the Lord. It's our responsibility to welcome others to meet Christ through us—through what we say and how we say it, the attitudes we project, the habits we carry, the actions we take, and those we choose not to take. These responsibilities are given to us as the Church, as people called to reflect our shared life with Christ. Accompanying these demands is the greatest joy and fulfillment we will ever know because they bring about the deepest realization of Christ present in and through the Church.

"*To accomplish so great a work, Christ is always present in his Church . . . .*"[5] So begins paragraph 7 of *Sacrosanctum concilium*. These are extraordinary words. It might be easy to read past them, given that what follows quickly points us to the fourfold presence of Christ in the Church's liturgical celebrations—that is, in the person of his minister, under the Eucharistic elements, in his Word, and in

4. "Video Message of His Holiness Pope Francis on the Occasion of the National Eucharistic Congress of India," November 12–15, 2015, www.vatican.va/content/francesco/en/messages/pont-messages/2015/documents/papa-francesco_20151112_messaggio-congresso-eucaristico-india.html.
5. SC, 7; emphasis added.

the liturgical assembly. However, before these four modes of Christ's presence in the liturgy are named, the Second Vatican Council stresses that Christ is always present in his Church. Not occasionally, not now and then but always—unceasingly, without interruption. Christ is present in his Church. In us! We who are the baptized community of believers, the Body of Christ, are the Church. And Christ is present in us. Yes, always. Even during those moments when we fall short of living up to who we are, Christ abides, tolerates us, and loves us into life. In our dying and rising with Christ in baptism, it is not we who live but Christ who lives in us.[6] This indwelling of Christ and the Holy Spirit turns us outward. Through the power of the Holy Spirit, we are bearers of Christ's continuing presence in this world.

A sacrament is "a visible sign of an invisible reality, a visible sign of an invisible grace."

—St. Augustine

The opening of paragraph 7 also makes clear the profound relationship between Christ's ongoing presence in the Church and the work of salvation—"*to accomplish so great a work*, Christ is always present in his Church."[7] This work of salvation is Christ and the Spirit present and active in the cosmos, in human life, guiding decisions and actions, moving individuals and communities to live in right relationships, healing and transforming all that is sinful and broken, and drawing the world into communion with a just and loving God. In the Catholic imagination, salvation is *gift*, freely given out of God's desire to share life with us. And because it's gift, we are invited to respond by becoming more fully human. Jesus shows us what it means to be human by dying to familiar human tendencies to be self-absorbed, in control, and the one holding the power. He made himself completely available and invited people

6. See Galatians 2:20.
7. SC, 7; emphasis added. See also *Catechism of the Catholic Church*, 1088, which explains "so great a work" referenced in paragraph 7 of SC as the "dispensation or communication of [Christ's] work of salvation."

who encountered him to come to new life. In the same way, we are called to turn away from thoughts, behaviors, and attitudes that are foolish, hateful, destructive, and ultimately lead to despair—whatever blocks life for ourselves, others, and the cosmos. We discover in Jesus Christ that we can trust God. We can trust that God desires for us to be freed from sin and come to *life*. The salvation offered to us in Christ is a process, a journey. It's a process of embracing the healing, reconciliation, and transformation that Christ makes possible. It's a journey of realizing the goodness of the world, the sacredness of life, and our interconnectedness with humanity and all of creation. It's an unfolding of live-giving, saving relationships that draw us more fully into divine communion.

As bearers of Christ's continuing presence, we share in the great work of salvation. God's act of self-giving continues to be visible in us as the Body of Christ living in the world. We are called to reflect in our own lives a life-grounding trust in God. We are to imitate the compassion, hospitality, and forgiveness of Jesus Christ. We are called to expend ourselves, bring others to life, and make concrete the life-giving relationships offered through Christ. We can do this work because Christ is "always present in his Church."[8]

Encountering the Presence of Christ

Being Attentive to the Daily Rhythms and Routines

On a chilly but sunny morning as I walked to work, I saw a gentleman sitting alone on the concrete of a small parking area. Everything he owned was stuffed in backpacks, and pieces of his cardboard sleeping mat were scattered around him. His hands were together, fingers tightly woven, lips moving, eyes cast down but looking skyward at times. "He's praying," I whispered to myself. As I walked toward him, I wondered, "What was his prayer? That today might be different? That he be visible to someone? That his needs for food and shelter be met? That he meet Christ in a passerby?" This man's

8. SC, 7.

presence to the Sacred Presence moved me deeply and evoked a profound awareness of Christ's presence *in him* and in our shared space of a city street. I met Christ in that moment and realized a oneness with this person. I was also invited to *be Christ* in that moment.

> **May [Christ's] peace grow strong in me, that I may bear the fruits of charity, justice, and truth.**
>
> —*Order of Baptism of Children*, 90

This encounter was gift. So too my attentiveness to it. The Holy Spirit ensured that this person grabbed my attention and stirred my heart. I further attribute my presence to this encounter with the Sacred in my daily routine to regular immersion in the Church's liturgy. Sunday after Sunday, I am rehearsed through the encounters with the presence of Christ in the assembly, the Word, the minister, and the Eucharist to become more present to Christ in the daily rhythms and routines. Our Sunday celebrations send us forth with a sharpened awareness of the daily invitations to encounter Christ and to be changed through these encounters. We should rush out of church shouting, "We are *present*, Lord!" We must be open to a continuous shaping and reshaping in our lives as Church in the world, and this happens when we are aware of and ready to meet Christ around every corner. It keeps us humble. We are reminded that Christ is at the center; Christ shapes the Church and makes it possible for us to be a visible sign of his presence in the world. Our showing up for the liturgy of life, attending to everyday moments as potentially revealing the Sacred, exercising our sacramental imagination, acting with integrity, and living with hope announces something about the Church. We proclaim our belief that the healing and transformative presence of Christ is met in the ordinary. Our own attentiveness to this presence makes us credible witnesses to Christ active and present in the world. The people whose path of life we cross may take note!

Putting on Our Church Behavior

"You need to put on your church behavior," my parents would sometimes say to my siblings and me on the way to Sunday Mass. Were these words simply a reminder that silliness in church would not be tolerated or something more? What I hear now in the echo of my parents' teaching is that we should put on our *Church* behavior day in and day out—to live in the world as Church. It is our responsibility as baptized persons to reveal Christ taking shape in the Church and in the world so others may encounter the presence of Christ in his Church, the Body of Christ, living in the world. *We become sacrament*, a visible sign of the Sacred Presence. In this way, we participate in the great work of salvation offered through Christ. Let us consider a few of the ways in which we as Church are the living sign of Christ's active and continuing presence.

Having a Sacramental Imagination

At a recent Sunday Mass, I noticed a four-year-old boy in his dad's arms. The boy had in one hand a dry brown leaf and in the other a droopy blade of ornamental grass. Such things could easily be overlooked or discarded as lifeless. But not for this child. With utter delight, he raised the leaf and blade of grass high in blessing, stretching his arms as far as he could as the Church sang the Gloria and "Holy, holy, holy," waving these precious things of the earth as though he were conducting the choir of angels in praising God for the beauty of creation. When Mass ended, he walked out clutching the leaf and blade of grass. They were infused with Divine Love, and the boy recognized their dignity. I saw in this young child an awesome sacramental imagination. He could see Grace in a fallen leaf and remnant of a plant. It also gave me hope. With such an imagination, I am hopeful that he will see that the devastation of the earth simply cannot be and become a voice for the planet, an advocate for the care of our common home. There is something inviting about a sacramental imagination, isn't there? We are drawn to someone who reveres the world and is present to the Sacred Presence.

A sacramental imagination is central to Catholic identity. It's the lens through which we look at life and the world. We see the world as inherently good; we look expectantly for experiences of the Sacred. We live anticipating that we will meet Grace, the gift of God's self-offering, in daily life. We recognize that, as the poet Gerard Manley Hopkins wrote, "[The] world is charged with the grandeur of God."[9] Even when faced with suffering or when we see evil, a sacramental imagination enables us to hold fast to hope and look for new life. God's loving outreach to the world will not be diminished.

Our participation in the Church's liturgical celebrations stretches and shapes this sacramental imagination. When we are sent forth on Sundays, we exercise this imagination in the liturgy of life as we engage with others in ways that value them, approach creation with reverence, and give witness to the incarnation—that is, God sharing life with us in Christ and the Holy Spirit. We become conscious of the possibility that those we meet may be drawn to us as a concrete expression of the Sacred Presence in the here and now. Let us then not overlook the dried brown leaves and broken blades of grass.

Living in Communion

"[The] Eucharist does not end with the partaking of the bread and blood of the Lord. It leads us to solidarity with others. The communion with the Lord is necessarily a communion with our fellow brothers and sisters."[10] Pope Francis' words point to our living in communion as another way in which the Church, nourished by the celebration of Eucharist, is a visible sign of the continuing presence of Christ. The invitations to live in communion with other persons and with the whole of creation occur daily. We are invited to see the poetry of people's lives, listen deeply to the lyrics of the cosmos,

9. From "God's Grandeur" by Gerard Manley Hopkins."
10. "Video Message of His Holiness Pope Francis on the Occasion of the National Eucharistic Congress of India," November 12–15, 2015.

and seek "common-union." Families and neighbors, friends and co-workers, people who cross our path of life in seemingly random ways all provide opportunities for living in communion. Extending hospitality to those in need—be they people who are struggling with illness, age, poverty, or addiction or families who are unhoused, seeking a new place to call home, in search of freedom and safety—reflects our commitment to sharing life with others. Our efforts to protect the planet, to stave off the impacts of climate change, to care for our forests and waterways, to look after the earth's creatures that bring us wonderment and joy proclaim to the world that our communion with the Lord means living in solidarity with the cosmos.

> **[We] want to be a Church that serves, that leaves home and goes forth from its places of worship, goes forth from its sacristies, in order to accompany life, to sustain hope, to be the sign of unity . . . to build bridges, to break down walls, to sow seeds of reconciliation.**
>
> —*Fratelli tutti*, 276

Pope Francis often emphasizes the need for the Church to learn the "'art of accompaniment,' which teaches us to remove our sandals before the sacred ground of the other (see Exodus 3:5)."[11] The willingness to accompany people *and* creation is a sure and certain sign of the effective presence of Christ in his Church as we live in the world. It becomes an invitation to others to meet Christ through our accompaniment and our living in solidarity with them and the created world.

Washing Feet

The Church is a community of foot washers. We rehearse this role at every celebration of the Eucharist when we are invited to "do this" in memory of Jesus Christ. The mandate to wash feet is ritualized in

11. *Evangelii gaudium*, 169.

a very poignant way during the Mass of the Lord's Supper on Holy Thursday. We know well the vivid scene in John's Gospel. Jesus assumes the role of servant and washes the feet of the disciples gathered at the table of the Last Supper. When he finished, he said to them,

> "Do you realize what I have done for you? You call me 'teacher' and 'master,' and rightly so, for indeed I am. If I, therefore, the master and teacher, have washed your feet, you ought to wash one another's feet. I have given you a model to follow, so that as I have done for you, you should also do."[12]

The mandate to wash feet is unique to John's Gospel. In Matthew, Mark, and Luke, Jesus invites his disciples at the Last Supper to reimagine ordinary bread and wine shared in common as something extraordinary—a foretaste of the heavenly banquet, a sacred sign of his continuing presence, and a symbol of their participation in the Divine Life. We hear in the Gospel accounts "Take and eat, take and drink, for this is my body, this is my blood."[13] In John's Gospel, however, these words do not appear; rather, the evangelist highlights the parallel action of Jesus deliberately and compassionately bending to meet the mundane. He reaches into the nooks and crannies of life and leans into the most soiled dimensions of humanity. John draws a clear connection between the sharing of the sacred meal and service. Jesus' command to be foot washers, servants in the world, should echo in our consciousness and be a guiding force for our daily choices and actions as persons and as Church.

Service is the general disposition of Christians, our way of being in the world. We are called to lead a profoundly sacrificial life, one in which we expend ourselves as Jesus did all his life. Such a life demands that we be self-forgetting and live for others. Paradoxically,

---

12. John 13:12–15.
13. Author's paraphrase; see Matthew 26:26–29; Mark 14:22–25; and Luke 22:14–20.

in living for others, we become more fully the persons and community God knows us to be.

Service is more than a one-time project or an activity we occasionally fit into our busy lives. It's daily. We wash feet in our homes and neighborhoods, workplaces and parish communities. We wash feet as we participate in recreational activities and social settings. We wash feet in our civic engagement and outreach to people near and far. Our attention to the well-being of others is also inextricably tied to the well-being of the planet. Clearly, washing feet includes caring for, protecting, and preserving our common home.

> **Christ's faithful . . . are to be the light of the world and to glorify the Father in the eyes of all.**
>
> —*Sacrosanctum concilium*, 9

Christ's ongoing presence in the Church enables our presence to the needs of humanity and the wider cosmos. We need to show up on a daily basis to see whose feet need to be washed. If we look the other way, are we really living the baptismal life that we share with Christ? If we shrug off our daily task of washing feet, do we really give meaning to what we celebrate when we gather for Mass? Showing up to wash feet might be as simple as holding the door for someone and making eye contact with them. Or it could be as involved as working with an organization that focuses on advocacy for people struggling to find affordable housing. Or maybe it means providing support to people who have had to flee their country to seek refuge where they can live freely and without fear. Or we may be called to ensure the full participation of persons of all abilities in the Church and society. Or we might wash the feet of our family members or neighbors who are elderly by driving them to an appointment or a grocery store. When we respond to the countless invitations to wash feet, we "announce the Gospel of the Lord." We are sent forth on Sundays with a clear mandate and are given what we need to do this work—a towel and a basin.

Working for Justice

A final piece for our consideration about ways in which we as Church are the living sign of Christ's active and continuing presence in the world is to reflect on our responsibility to advance justice. Justice is a kind of connective tissue; it is knitted into the Catholic sacramental imagination, our desire to live in communion with others and the planet, and the giving of ourselves in service. Justice is a habit of heart formed and sustained through active participation in the liturgy of the Church *and* the liturgy of life.

The justice we speak about here is the *justice of God*. Justice is another name for God; it is who God is—self-giving and desirous of sharing life with humanity and creation. God invites humanity into a web of life-giving relationships with the Divine, one another, and the created world. As Christians, we believe Jesus Christ definitively embodies Divine self-giving in relationship with all God has brought into being. As the Body of Christ, as people who share in the life of a just God and who are a visible sign of Christ's continuing presence in the Church and in the world, our mission is one of justice. Thus, the world meets the justice of God revealed in Christ as it meets us.

How might we carry out this mission of justice? We can first point back to the need for a sacramental imagination. A sacramental imagination has no place for injustices. For instance, the exploitation of people or the environment, violence, poverty, inequality, prejudices, and bullying that denigrate persons obscure the just reign of God and thus are an offense to the Catholic sacramental imagination. Anything that harms or destroys right relationships belies the innate goodness of the people and things of this world and is thus intolerable.

As people called to live in communion, we appreciate that we are wired to bring others to life. We extend to others what centers us—the justice of God revealed in Jesus Christ. This may mean helping others to discover their inherent dignity and giftedness, lifting up those who feel discouraged or broken and giving them